Love and Death on Long Island

Love and Death on Long Island

A screenplay by Richard Kwietniowski

Based on the novel by Gilbert Adair

SCREENPRESS BOOKS

First published in 1998
by ScreenPress Books
28 Castle Street Eye Suffolk
IP23 7AW

Photoset by Parker Typesetting Service, Leicester
Printed in England by Clays Ltd, St Ives plc.

Screenplay developed by Alfalfa Entertainments
in association with Skyline Productions
with the support of British Screen Finance

Production stills: Sophie Baker (UK), Chris Reardon (Can)
Storyboard: Paul Ruxton & James L. Wolstenholme
Music score: Richard Grassby-Lewis (composer), David Lyon (orchestrator)

A CIP record for this book
is available from the British Library

ISBN 1 901680 08 8

For more information on forthcoming ScreenPress Books,
contact the publishers at:

ScreenPress Books
28 Castle Street
Eye, Suffolk
IP23 7AW
fax: 01379 870 267
email: screenpressbooks@hotmail.com

Contents

BOOK > *SCRIPT* > FILM

The film script is a unique phenomenon. Before shooting, it's never considered finished, and afterwards it bears only a ghostly relationship to the film that replaces it. Yet it remains the industry's most important commodity, with many functions.

The text that follows is, word for word, the fifth and final draft of *Love and Death on Long Island*. It's exactly what was read by John Hurt in Kenya, Jason Priestley in Los Angeles, Maury Chaykin in Toronto and Sheila Hancock in London. It's what eleven backers in the UK, Canada and Italy eventually committed to, and also what crews on both sides of the Atlantic prepared, in infinitesimal detail, for shooting. It seems crazy to expect any one document to fulfil such a diversity of roles, but that's the way it works.

Although I tried to follow Preston Sturges' dictum of doing most of the directing in the writing, the script inevitably differs from the film. It includes scenes omitted from the final cut (due only to its relentless logic) and lacks the verve and sensibility brought to it by an exceptional cast and crew. It now seems something frozen in time, a projection of what the film might be, containing more and less than it in equal measure. It bears the same relationship to the novel it is based on, a cornucopia of delights that I first read by chance in Bristol on a balmy night in July 1990.

Thus began the biggest adventure of my life, almost as big as that of the film's central character. I wish the book/script/film could be as enriching to all who come into contact with them.

Richard Kwietniowski
London, April 1998

Love and Death on Long Island

Titles over waves breaking on the sand.

EXT. A LONG ISLAND BEACH – DAY

Footprints in the sand lead to a young man (Ronnie) walking his dog back to a powder-blue Porsche.

EXT. CHESTERTON, LONG ISLAND – DAY

The day begins in an affluent neighbourhood surrounded by woodland.

The Mailman leaves his jeep to make deliveries; an elderly jogger passes by; a woman walks her dog; a boy hurls papers into front gardens from his bike; kids hurry to a school-bus.

As Ronnie returns home, a delivery is made to his mailbox.

A voice-over begins as we travel steadily towards the mailbox and into it, to black.

> GILES
> *(voice-over)*
> It is so difficult to know where I should begin; especially when, unlike you, I already know the ending. But let us say that this story began with the end of another, far, far from the surf of Long Island . . .

EXT. PORTLAND PLACE, LONDON – DAY

We travel out of a red London pillar-box, to reveal Broadcasting House across the busy street.

> GILES
> *(voice-over)*
> For many years I had absolutely no public life. I had said 'No' to interviews so often, it was widely regarded as my forte. Then, just once, on impulse I said 'Yes' . . .

INT. A RECORDING STUDIO, LONDON – DAY

Giles and his interviewer are isolated from the production team by glass.

> ELDRIDGE
> You remain something of an enigma, despite this resurgence of interest in your work.

> GILES
> I believe so.

> ELDRIDGE
> You don't think your readers have the right to know a little about you?

> GILES
> I have no idea who my readers are, so . . .

> ELDRIDGE
> Really? None at all?

> GILES
> Well, people like myself, I suppose.

> ELDRIDGE
> (*amused*)
> So who do you write for?

> GILES
> Myself!

Pause.

> ELDRIDGE
> Does popular – or critical – acclaim mean nothing to you?

> GILES
> Practically nothing.

> ELDRIDGE
> May I ask why you're here today?

GILES

I was wondering that myself, but I was asked with a great
degree of charm . . .

He smiles at the producer. She looks tense.

Your, er, colleague knew my late wife, who translated for the
World Service, and I do have a faint curiosity about how these
things are done, you know.

INT. GILES' STUDY – DAY

*A photograph of his late wife sits on the mantelpiece, beside an
old-fashioned wireless. Giles listens to the broadcast with an
increasingly pained expression.*

*On his desk lies a book of French poetry, a beautiful fountain-pen,
a notebook and a Sunday paper folded open on radio listings. Its
description of him comes to fill the frame:* '4p.m. Wordsmiths.
Interview with Giles De'Ath, erstwhile fogey, now cult.'

ELDRIDGE
(*voice-over, from radio*)
You've never been tempted to write for radio? Or television?

GILES

I'm afraid not.

ELDRIDGE

Would you permit your work to be adapted for the screen,
now that even E. M. Forster's been done?

GILES

I'd prefer not to be done.

ELDRIDGE

But he's been done rather well, don't you think?

GILES

I have no idea. I haven't been to the pictures for quite some
time.

5

Pause.

                    ELDRIDGE
Does the twentieth century play any part in your life?

                     GILES
I'm sorry?

                    ELDRIDGE
Do you, for instance, use a word processor?

Pause.

                     GILES
I'm a writer. I write. I don't process words.

Giles emphatically switches the radio off.

EXT. GILES' HOUSE – DAY

Giles closes the front door before noticing he still has his slippers on. He comes back out in shoes but cannot find his keys. Peering through the letterbox, he sees them inside. A tremor of panic crosses his face.

EXT. PHONE BOX – DAY

As Giles waits for a young couple to finish their call, it starts to rain. He taps the glass. They look disdainfully at him.

EXT. CINEMA ENTRANCE – DAY

Giles shelters from the rain with others. A bus passes, revealing only Giles remaining. He glances idly through grimy glass at the film poster: E. M. Forster's Eternal Moment.

He relishes the coincidence, then fights the temptation to succumb. As if to settle the matter he glances up at the downpour.

1. Cinema 1

INT. CINEMA FOYER – DAY

In the ticket booth a woman's head comes into view as she picks up a ball of wool.

> TICKET SELLER
>
> One or two?

Giles looks to either side, to indicate he is alone.

> GILES
> *(confused)*
>
> One.

The machine spews out a ticket with ONE *on it.*

INT. CINEMA AUDITORIUM – DAY

Giles feels his way to a seat at the front, some distance from the sparse audience.

The noise of motorbikes and rock music subsides as he fumbles for his glasses.

On screen:

EXT. DORMITORY – NIGHT

Four American teenage boys hide in bushes beside a college building.

> BRAD
>
> Are you sure it's the right window, man?

> TOMMY
>
> I don't like this, Corey. What if we get caught?

> COREY
>
> We're not gonna get caught, jerk-off. And any minute now that room's gonna be full of butt-naked babes.

BIG GUY

Alright.

COREY

Gimme the camera, Big Guy.

Assuming he is watching a trailer, Giles grimaces at its lewd banality.

On screen, a matronly Teacher stops jogging and performs bizarre leg-stretching exercises.

Back at the dorm, Corey videos two girls undressing in one of the rooms.

BIG GUY

Oh, man, I'm drooling . . .

COREY

Shit! There's a light flashing.

TOMMY

Battery's going.

BRAD

It's overheating, like me.

COREY

Come on, babe, show me what you got.

BIG GUY

She is so totally hot.

Giles indignantly checks his watch in the light of the screen.

TOMMY

Hey! Someone's coming!

Corey re-frames the camera on the Teacher charging towards them.

COREY

Christ, it's The Stomper.

TOMMY

I'm outta here.

TEACHER
(*German accent*)
Vot are you boys doink heer? You shouldn't be heer.

Big Guy remains transfixed by the girls in the window. The Teacher dives and pins him to the ground.

BIG GUY

Oooooof!

GILES
(*indignant*)
This isn't E. M. Forster!

He turns to the rest of the audience who merely snigger at the scene.

On screen:

EXT. A PIZZA PARLOR – DAY

Brad brings food out to Tommy and Corey who sit in a battered convertible.

BRAD

Hey, man, you got yourself a rival. Molly's inside – with a guy!

COREY
(*getting out of the car*)
I'll kill him.

On screen:

INT. PIZZA PARLOR – DAY

Molly's frothy hair conceals the face of the boy whose hand she clutches.

*The faces of Brad, Tommy, Corey and Big Guy rise into view,
peering through a window.*

COREY

. . . Mikey!?

TOMMY

You've been beaten to it by your kid brother.

BRAD

Looks to me like they've gone all the way, too.

COREY

Shut up, Brad. It's time for a pizza delivery.

*Corey enters the Parlour and throws a pizza across the room like a
frisbee. It whirls through the air like a flying saucer before
splattering onto Ronnie's chest.*

Giles seizes his coat and stands up.

RONNIE
(*standing up on screen*)

Hey. Cut it out!

*He wears a kitchen-worker's apron and hat, and has a vulnerable,
almost delicate appearance.*

Oh. Hi, Corey. What's up?

Giles pauses momentarily.

COREY

Your little pecker, by the look of it!

RONNIE

Corey, can we talk about this?

*Corey pulls Ronnie to the ground where they roll around. Molly
looks on, delighted.*

BRAD
(from the window)

Go, dude, go.

Suddenly intrigued, Giles sinks back into his seat, as Ronnie is easily overcome and shoved onto a table.

RONNIE

Corey, she made me . . .

COREY

Shut up, you little jerk-off.

Giles watches with appalled delight as Corey squirts ketchup from a plastic tomato up Ronnie's apron and onto his face. Ronnie lies sobbing in an almost classical pose. One arm drops to the floor, scattering napkins.

Isolated sniggers come from the audience, but Giles is transfixed; the scene is imbued with a significance beyond the plotline.

INT. CINEMA FOYER – DAY

Giles tiptoes out. The Ticket Seller and Usherette look up from the booth where they are winding a ball of wool.

EXT. CINEMA ENTRANCE – DAY

The display clearly indicates a twin-screen cinema: 1. Hotpants College II; 2. Eternal Moment.

Giles looks at the gaudy Hotpants College II *poster. In the background of the depicted beach party stands a partially obscured Ronnie, a minor character.*

EXT. PHONE-BOX – DAY

GILES

And when will she return from Whitstable? . . . Oh dear. Maybe a neighbour has a spare set of keys.

INT. MRS REED'S LIVING-ROOM – NIGHT

Giles' neighbour brings the keys into a room dominated by family photographs. She is deaf.

GILES

What a relief. My wife must have known this would happen.

Mrs Reed, nods unsurely, lip-reading.

We haven't seen too much of each other since her . . .

MRS REED

Never.

GILES

I'm sorry?

MRS REED

I not see you.

GILES

We've both been busy, I suppose.

MRS REED

Busy for a long time!

GILES
(glancing at the TV)
Tell me, Mrs Reed, don't you live here alone now?

MRS REED

Yes. Me alone.

GILES

But the television?

MRS REED

Mine. I like it.

GILES

You . . . watch the pictures?

MRS REED
(*pressing her remote control*)
With subtitles.

On TV screen, with subtitles.

INT. TV STUDIO – DAY

QUIZ-MASTER
Your specialist subject is Christopher Columbus. You have two minutes, starting *now*: by what name was Columbus known in Spain?

CONTESTANT
Christobol Colon.

QUIZ-MASTER
Correct. Of what did Columbus reputedly become the first European connoisseur?

CONTESTANT
. . . Tobacco?

Mrs Reed flips the TV off.

GILES
How extraordinary.

She indicates that she did not see his mouth.

I'm sorry; ve-ry cle-ver.

MRS REED
Yes, clever. Tea?

GILES
Thank you, no. I have a cold supper waiting.

MRS REED
You locked out all day?

GILES

No, no. Only a short while. I went to the pictures.

She shakes her head.

Ci-ne-ma.

MRS REED

Good?

GILES

Execrable.

She shakes her head again.

Very bad. I saw the wrong film.

INT. GILES' HOUSE – DAY

His housekeeper brings coffee and biscuits into the imposing study.
Giles is answering correspondence at his desk.

MRS BARKER

I'm ever so sorry about yesterday.

GILES

And why is that?

MRS BARKER

About not being home, when you needed the keys.

GILES

I can hardly dictate what you do on Sundays, Mrs Barker.

MRS BARKER

My sister in Whitstable's been poorly. Needs a bit of helping
out.

GILES

The crisis prompted me to renew my acquaintance with Mrs
Reed. Gwen knew her quite well, as I recall.

MRS BARKER
She copes terribly well, Mrs Reed.

GILES
You, er, communicate with her?

MRS BARKER
Oh yes. Round the back.

She picks up the Sunday paper.

I take it this is finished with?

GILES
I shall be lunching out today.

MRS BARKER
(*hovering*)
That's nice.

GILES
Is there, anything else, Mrs Barker?

MRS BARKER
I was just going to mention . . . My sister and I heard you on
the radio yesterday.

INT. A RESTAURANT – DAY

GILES
Is it a crime, Henry, to say that one doesn't write in order to
be read?

HENRY
Well, it won't exactly shift volumes!

GILES
It wasn't my intention to be . . . difficult. You know.

HENRY
(*smiling*)
But that *is* your reputation, Giles.

16

GILES

D'you know, there were even people listening in Whitstable?

HENRY

I should hope so too.

GILES

Tell me, you were never taught by Forster, when you were up at Cambridge?

HENRY

Alas, no.

GILES

You know, they're even adapting his work for the pictures now? I can't say that I approve.

HENRY

It could have been a lot worse.

GILES

The adaptation?

HENRY

The interview.

GILES

In what way?

HENRY

It could have been on television. Now that would have been a much greater intrusion, I can tell you.

GILES

Did you know, Henry, you can get televisions which transcribe what people say?

EXT. A LONDON STREET – DAY

Giles' attention is drawn from the window of an antiquarian bookshop to a burger-bar. A plastic tomato sits on each table. He frowns as something stirs in his memory.

INT. GILES' KITCHEN – NIGHT

Giles finishes his prepared meal. On top of a dish put over another is a label with the word 'Desert' on it. He takes out his pen and adds the missing 'S'. With a dash of ceremony, he removes the top dish. There is nothing underneath it.

INT./EXT. GILES' HOUSE – DAY

From the kitchen, we see Mrs Barker in the garden talking to Mrs Reed over the fence.

> MRS BARKER
>
> Well, that's just it, isn't it?

She fails to hear the door bell.

> Every time I go there, they're never open.

The bell rings again. Giles opens the front door irritably, revealing a helmeted, gladiatorial figure.

> GILES
>
> Good lord.

A package and clipboard are thrust at him.

> Ah. The proofs.

INT. GILES' STUDY – DAY

Giles finishes lunch, studying the proofs.

> MRS BARKER
> (*taking the tray*)
> May I ask, would that be another book?

> GILES
>
> I'm afraid it is, yes.

> MRS BARKER
>
> I don't know how you do it. It takes me an age to read one.

GILES

Ah, yes, well. Gwen always used to say that it's easier to write one than read one properly.

MRS BARKER

I'm sure she did. I can almost hear her saying it.

She scowls at the photograph of his late wife on the mantelpiece.

INT. A STEAM BATHS – DAY

Giles grimaces in pain as an ageing masseur methodically pounds his back, the words 'love' and 'hate' tattooed on his knuckles.

INT. GILES' STUDY – DAY

MRS BARKER
(*cautiously answering the phone*)

Hello . . .? Oh, no. He has his steam bath today, then he'll be taking his walk. Always back by six, though.

She opens the first few pages of the proofs as if buried treasure lay there.

EXT. HAMPSTEAD HEATH – DUSK

On his walk, Giles is deep in thought. We hear stray lines from Ronnie's dialogue:

RONNIE
(*voice-over*)

Oh. Hi, Corey. What's up?

Giles spots Mrs Reed with her dog and tries to avoid her.

INT. MRS REED'S LIVING ROOM – NIGHT

MRS REED
(*pointing to her 'minicom' phone*)

Telephone.

                    GILES
Oh, really?

                    MRS REED
                  (*pouring tea*)
I type; they read. I'm a chatterbox.

                    GILES
Remarkable.

Mrs Reed hovers with the sugar tongs.

                    MRS REED
One or two?

INT. GILES' BEDROOM – NIGHT

                    GILES
              (*reading the proofs*)
Aha!

He triumphantly unscrews the lid of his fountain-pen and arrows a gap that drops between words in an unbroken line down the whole page.

INT. TATE GALLERY – DAY

Giles and a haughty woman about his age pause in front of Wallis' portrait of the young poet Chatterton. It bears an uncanny resemblance to Ronnie's final pose in the pizza parlor. Giles is struck by the similarity.

                    MAUREEN
I've never really approved of the Pre-Raphaelites.

                    GILES
Mmm?

                    MAUREEN
Well, just look at him.

GILES
(*smiling*)
This was one of your sister's favourites.

MAUREEN
What's meant to be going on? Love letters; suicide; that sort of thing?

GILES
They're more likely to be rejections from publishers. Chatterton was a writer.

MAUREEN
(*walking on*)
I must get around to reading one of *your* books, Giles. There never seem to be enough hours in the day . . .

Giles lingers. We hear an echo from the film:

RONNIE
(*voice-over*)
Corey . . . She made me . . .

MAUREEN
Giles?

INT. GILES' HOUSE – DAY

On his study desk lies a Sunday paper, the proof page with the typographical quirk and a postcard of the Chatterton portrait.

GILES
(*voice-over, writing*)
Winsome; young; neo-classical? Isolated – by beauty? DEAF?

He closes the notebook and arranges everything on the desk at right angles.

In the kitchen, as a clock strikes, he places a casserole in the oven according to Mrs Barker's instructions.

Back in his study, he idly flicks on the radio.

> ELDRIDGE
> (*voice-over*)
> Welcome to 'Wordsmiths'. I'm Steven Eldridge, and this week we're looking at codes of masculinity in the novels of Kingsley Amis.

Giles hurriedly switches it off and opens the paper by chance on the cinema page.

> GILES
> Oh, bugger it.

EXT. THE CINEMA ENTRANCE – DAY

Giles stands outside, confounded. Hotpants College II *has been replaced by* Improper Advances. Eternal Moment *plays on.*

EXT. PHONE BOX – DAY

Giles dials a number in a listings magazine. An effete young man answers.

> JASON
> (*voice-over*)
> MGM Hammersmith, Jason speaking.

> GILES
> I wonder, could you tell me where you are?

> JASON
> In the box office, sir.

Giles' eyes hit the ceiling.

EXT. TAXI – DAY

Giles lights a cigarette. The Driver swings back the glass partition.

                    TAXI DRIVER
No smoking, guv, thank you very much.

                    GILES
I beg your pardon?

                    TAXI DRIVER
It says 'No Smoking'.

                    GILES
No, it says 'Thank You For Not Smoking'. As I'm smoking, I
don't expected to be thanked.

EXT. A MULTIPLEX CINEMA – DAY

The cinema's billing boasts Hotpants College II (18), *with* The
Heat Is On (PG), Uncle Ed (U), *and* Pulse (15).

INT. MULTIPLEX CINEMA – DAY

Jason stands guard in the ticket booth.

                    GILES
                   (*carefully*)
One for number three.

                    JASON
Come again?

                    GILES
One adult for number three.

                    JASON
What do you want to see, Sir?

                    GILES
The film in number three.

                    JASON
Which?

GILES
(*reluctantly*)
'Hotpants College Two'.

JASON
(*triumphantly*)
Thank you!

INT. MULTIPLEX AUDITORIUM – DAY

Two layers of curtains rise noisily. The screen is illuminated with the proud announcement: 'This Is A No Smoking Cinema'.

The curtains lower as the lights fade up with accompanying 'mambo' music, only to fade down again almost immediately. The curtains rise to reveal the censor's certificate. Giles watches, bewildered.

EXT. A COLLEGE – DAY

To rock music, opening titles for Hotpants College II *over:*

Girl students meet, chatter and consult their books in the elegant courtyard. Two Teachers, The Stomper and a gaunt, bespectacled schoolmarm, march the girls towards the road.

Brad, Tommy and Big Guy drive a battered convertible into the college.

The Teachers suddenly pause in horror as the boys moon at them from the passing car. The girls all giggle as the gaunt teacher faints into the arms of The Stomper.

Whooping with laughter, the guys drive on to a modest family home: Corey's house . . .

EXT./INT. COREY'S HOUSE – DAY

In the kitchen, Corey drinks milk from the carton, whilst his long-suffering Mother prepares breakfast. A car horn sounds.

COREY

Gotta go, Mom. Today's a real big day.

MOTHER

Oh yeah? What's so special about it?

COREY

The college girls are back, that's what.

Ronnie enters, listening to a Walkman.

MOTHER

I wish you'd keep your mind on school, Corey, like your brother.
(*smoothing Ronnie's hair*)
If he finds time to work at Chicken Burger, why can't you?

The screen throws a play of light on Giles' face as he reacts to Ronnie's introduction with an awed enthusiasm.

Time-lapses establish his alternating responses: bored distaste and rapt delight.

On screen, we again see the end of the pizza parlor scene with Ronnie in the Chatterton pose.

On screen:

CREDIT ROLLER

In the film's cast list, Ronnie's name seems slightly more illuminated than the others:

Mikey . . . . RONNIE BOSTOCK

INT. GILES' HOUSE – NIGHT

Giles enters the darkened hall, sniffing. In the kitchen, he opens the oven to release a cloud of smoke.

INT. GILES' STUDY – DAY

                  GILES
           (*voice-over, writing*)
Ronnie Bostock. R. Bostock Esq. Bostock (Ronald).

             MRS BARKER
       (*knocking and entering*)
I thought I should ask what happened to the casserole . . .

                  GILES
It was entirely my fault. I . . . took a longer walk than usual.

Pause.

             MRS BARKER
No harm done, was there?

INT. THE RESTAURANT – DAY

                HENRY
A film actor? Good Lord! Which one?

                  GILES
Oh, no one in particular.

                HENRY
I had no idea you went to the cinema, Giles.

                  GILES
I don't, Henry. That's why I'm asking you this question.

                HENRY
You want to know how to find the filmography of an actor?

                  GILES
Or actress.

INT. GILES' KITCHEN – NIGHT

After supper, Giles flicks despondently through film magazines. He pounces on a brief review

GILES
(*voice-over, reading*)
Hotpants College II: puerile romp without a single redeeming feature.

He sweeps the magazines angrily off the table, tipping the milk onto the floor.

INT. GROCERY SHOP – NIGHT

It is a family-run late-night store, the 'Aphrodite'.

GILES
You wouldn't have any milk left, I suppose?

The teenage girl behind the counter stops reading and steps sullenly into a back room behind the shop.

ABIGAIL
Mum – milk.

Giles glances at the upside-down page of her magazine on the counter.

GIRL'S MOTHER
(*with a Greek accent*)
UHT?

He mouths the letters as if they were some sort of code. As she disappears, he spins the magazine round. Amongst the brightly-coloured text is a small but unmistakable photograph of Ronnie. The woman returns and puts a carton of UHT milk on top of it.

Only this left. Is OK?

GILES
It's milk, isn't it?

GIRL'S MOTHER
Abigail? We close now.

GILES

There was something else I wanted.

ABIGAIL

We're closing now.

GILES

I shan't be long.

He moves behind a shelf, ready to pounce. Yawning, she picks up the magazine and closes it. Giles grabs a bottle of ketchup.

Here we are.

Abigail slaps the magazine on the counter, revealing the title Sugar.

INT. GILES' KITCHEN – DAY

Mrs Barker makes a cup of tea. She takes the bottle of ketchup from the fridge and holds it up to the light.

EXT. A PAPER STAND – DAY

Giles deftly takes copies of Sugar *and* Motoring Monthly *off the stand, pays, and rolls them tightly into a tube.*

INT. GILES' STUDY – DAY

Giles stands motionless in front of the mirror as we hear Mrs Barker leave. Out of habit, he straightens his tie and checks his cuff links.

GILES
(*looking at Gwen's photograph*)
What on earth am I up to?

He sits down at the desk and takes the magazines from a drawer. Motoring Monthly *is immediately binned, but he pores, intrigued, over* Sugar's *photo-stories, agony-aunt page and adverts for make-up, tampons and acne cures.*

(*voice-over, reading*)
Out soon on video, *Hotpants College II* has even more
yummy guys than *HCI*, including mega dream-boat Ronnie
Bostock. Next month, find out how 'Bostie' fares in our
feature on Hollywood's Most Snoggable Fellas. Exclamation
mark. Exclamation mark. Exclamation mark.

INT. THE GROCERY SHOP – NIGHT

Abigail is reading another magazine, Big. *As a carton of UHT milk
is placed on the counter, she looks up and smiles.*

INT. A NEWSAGENTS – DAY

*Giles waits for two girls to leave, then swiftly gathers up a copy of
every teenage magazine. The newsagent looks at him twice.*

INT. GILES' KITCHEN – DAY

*Mrs Barker finishes peeling potatoes over the cover of the
motoring magazine.*

INT. GILES' STUDY – DAY

*Giles uses scissors to cut a picture from one of the magazines. On
hearing the knock, he sweeps everything into a drawer.*

> MRS BARKER
> Sorry to disturb you, but I've looked everywhere for them,
> and . . .

> GILES
> Mrs Barker, I think it would be best if I were left
> uninterrupted in the afternoons. My work is very taxing at
> present.

> MRS BARKER
> What about your tea?

GILES

I'll call you when I'm ready for it. It's been a bit odd this week,
I must say.

MRS BARKER

It's that funny milk

GILES

Ah. Now what is it you can't find?

MRS BARKER

The kitchen scissors.

EXT. HAMPSTEAD HEATH – NIGHT

*Giles stealthily deposits remnants of the magazines into a
brimming litter-bin.*

EXT./INT. A SOHO NEWSAGENTS – DAY

*Giles chooses teenage magazines carefully, checking each contents
page and fold-out poster. The newsagent puts them in a brown
paper bag as if they were pornography.*

INT. GILES' HOUSE – DAY

*A staple is carefully removed from a fold-out pin-up of Ronnie.
Scissors cut out an interview. Pictures are laid out on the desk
according to repeated outfits and props, especially a decorated
guitar, a large shaggy dog and a powder-blue Porsche.*

*Intercut with these are fragments of Giles' week: newsagents'
windows; Giles' shoulder kneaded by the hand with 'love'
tattooed on; a brimming litter-bin on the Heath; a pint of UHT
milk landing on the counter; cuttings stuck in an old-fashioned
scrapbook.*

7: **Bostockiana A**

GILES
(*voice-over, writing*)
Skid Marks (1994). Tex Mex (1995). Hotpants College II (1996).

He closes the book, writes 'Bostockiana' on the cover, and locks it in the drawer.

(*into the hall*)
Mrs Barker? I'll take tea now.

He approaches the kitchen.

Mrs Barker?

He stops, perturbed, as he hears her in the garden.

MRS BARKER
I think he's doing something for the pictures, 'cos he was reading up about the films the other week, *and* he's thinking of buying a car!

MRS REED
Really?

MRS BARKER
Doesn't sound like him at all, does it? And you know what parking's like round here.

INT. GILES' STUDY – NIGHT

Dressed for bed, Giles sits in an armchair with a brandy, browsing through the scrapbook. One page features images of Ronnie without a shirt. A large mole on his neck is on the right in some; on the left in others.

GILES
Is it on the left, or the right?

INT. GILES' BEDROOM – NIGHT

Giles lies in bed. A beam of cinematic light from a street lamp penetrates the darkness. He answers questions as if on the quiz show he saw on Mrs Reed's television:

INT. TV STUDIO – DAY

QUIZ-MASTER

What is your specialist subject?

GILES

The life and work of Ronnie Bostock.

QUIZ-MASTER

You have two minutes, starting now. Ronnie Bostock was born in southern California, but where does he live now?

GILES

Chesterton, Long Island.

QUIZ-MASTER

Correct. What is the name of his dog which figures prominently in publicity stills?

GILES

Strider.

QUIZ-MASTER

Correct. What is Ronnie Bostock's favourite reading material?

GILES

Stephen King and science-fiction.

QUIZ-MASTER

Correct. What does Ronnie have a self-confessed weakness for?

Pause.

GILES

Pizza.

I'll accept that. It's pizza with extra anchovies. Of which actor would he give his right arm to play the son?

GILES

Jack Nicholson.

QUIZ-MASTER

Correct. Under what circumstances would Ronnie do a nude scene?

GILES

If it were tasteful?

QUIZ-MASTER

And . . . ?

GILES

Essential to the plot.

QUIZ-MASTER

Correct. Why was he *not* cast in the original *Hotpants College*?

GILES

Er . . . too young?

QUIZ-MASTER

No! He was unable to break his contract with the sitcom 'Home Is Where The Heart Is'. What is Ronnie's favourite kind of training shoe, and why?

GILES

Reebok, because British stuff is 'cool'.

QUIZ-MASTER

Correct. Which of his rock idols was he recently photographed with?

GILES
(*authoritatively*)

Axl Rose.

QUIZ-MASTER

Correct. Ronnie claims he likes nothing better than 'hanging out with the guys'. What exactly do these 'guys' mean to him?

GILES
(*pausing, perturbed*)

I wonder . . .

INT. THE GROCERY SHOP – DAY

A brand of cigarettes catches Giles' eye.

GILES

Oh. Chesterton, is that?

GIRL'S MOTHER

Chesterton? You want?

GILES

Why not?

GIRL'S MOTHER

For a change, yes?

INT. THE RESTAURANT – DAY

HENRY

I have as usual said you're far too busy, but it is a very prestigious lecture, you know.

GILES

Would you advise me against it?

HENRY

As your agent, I'd strongly urge you to do it. As a friend, I wouldn't like anything to disturb your work, which seems to be so . . . invigorating, Giles.

39

Pause.

> GILES

Let me think about it.

> HENRY

Really?

> GILES

I'm growing a little tired of hearing myself say no.

Henry beams at him in surprise.

> Now, Henry, I need a little help . . . What exactly is a
> 'sitcom'?

EXT. HAMPSTEAD HEATH – DUSK

*Giles checks his watch and stages a surprise meeting with Mrs
Reed.*

> GILES

Hello! How nice to bump into you . . . You're looking
extremely well. May I carry something for you?

To his dismay, she hands him the dog's lead.

INT. MRS REED'S LIVING ROOM – NIGHT

Giles accepts a cup of tea with a degree of impatience.

> GILES

May I have another look at your television with the words?

> MRS REED

Television?

*She presses the remote control, revealing a sheepdog trials
programme.*

> GILES
> *(seizing the remote control))*

This is very clever.

> MRS REED

Yes. You can sit. All night.

> GILES

Extraordinary.

He presses the remote experimentally and beams with pleasure when the programme changes to 'Home Is Where The Heart Is'.

On TV:

INT. TV STUDIO KITCHEN – DAY

> MOTHER

Chip, go tell your father he's taking you bowling tonight.

> RONNIE

Oh, Mom; why can't I ever give him good news?

Canned laughter.

> MOTHER

Because I tell him that myself.

Canned laughter.

On TV:

INT. TV STUDIO GARAGE – DAY

> RONNIE

Hi, Dad. Hey, the car looks great.

> FATHER

How's it going, Chip?

> RONNIE

Hey, Dad; what about bowling tonight?

                              FATHER
Oh boy.

                              RONNIE
What's wrong?

                              FATHER
What have I done to get Mom mad?

Canned laughter.

                            MRS REED
                      (*reclaiming the remote*)
No good, this programme.

                              GILES
                        (*a little hurt*)
Really?

Mrs Reed flicks back to the sheepdog trials.

                            MRS REED
This is better. Dogs.

Giles winces in frustration.

You like dogs too?

INT. A TELEVISION SHOP – DAY

Giles examines a row of microwave ovens.

                            ASSISTANT
Need any help, sir?

                              GILES
Yes. I'm interested in acquiring a video player.

                            ASSISTANT
These are microwaves, sir. Videos are over here . . . Let's start
with this little humdinger. It's got it all, this one. Nicam digital
stereo, long-play facility, fourteen day eight-event timer, two-
speed slow-motion . . .

GILES

My needs are rather limited.

ASSISTANT

It's top of the range, this one.

GILES

Oh, is it?

ASSISTANT

And it's in your interests to keep up with technology.

GILES

What was that about slow motion?

INT. GILES' HOUSE – DAY

The door bell rings. Giles flies out of his study.

GILES

I'll get it, Mrs Barker.

ROB

Delivery for Doctor Death.

GILES
(*wearily*)

Yes.

ROB

Is that your real name, then?

GILES

It's pronounced Day-aa-th.

ROB

Get a lot of jokes, do you?

INT. GILES' STUDY – DAY

> ROB
> (*cheekily*)
> Nice place, this. All them books; they're not all different, are they?

> GILES
> Could we, er . . .

> ROB
> Oh yeah, right. Where's your telly?

> GILES
> My what?

> ROB
> Gogglebox. TV. Not in here, is it?

> GILES
> I don't have one.

> ROB
> Blimey. What's this for, then?

> GILES
> For watching films on, actually.

> ROB
> But what you gonna watch 'em on?

> GILES
> (*unsurely*)
> On the video?

> ROB
> Man, I don't believe this.

Mrs Barker listens outside the door.

INT. A VIDEO-RENTAL SHOP – NIGHT

Giles lays his passport on the counter of what might be an airport check-in.

> GILES
>
> Two pieces of identification and one proof of address. I believe that qualifies me for membership?

> VIDEO SHOP ASSISTANT
>
> There's a ten quid deposit so you don't nick nothing, but you get a two quid voucher for Bernie's pizza deliveries. You can take two tapes out now if you want.

> GILES
>
> I was rather hoping for three.

> VIDEO SHOP ASSISTANT
>
> You'd be up all night if you took three, wouldn't you?

> GILES
>
> Couldn't I forfeit my Bernie's pizza voucher for a third one?

In the 'comedy' section, Giles finds Skid Marks, *then crosses the aisle to 'action' for* Tex Mex.

> VIDEO SHOP ASSISTANT
>
> That's out.

> GILES
>
> I'm sorry?

> VIDEO ASSISTANT
>
> *Tex Mex.* Went out an hour ago.

> GILES
>
> Really?

> VIDEO SHOP ASSISTANT
>
> We've only got one of everything unless it's a blockbuster.

GILES
(*confused*)
I see.

VIDEO SHOP ASSISTANT
That's in. Harry – *Skid Marks*?

HARRY
(*from the stacks*)
No. Tape's buggered.

VIDEO SHOP ASSISTANT
Not your night, is it? You want to have another bash?

GILES
(*mustering his courage*)
Perhaps you might have . . . *Hotpants College Two*?

VIDEO SHOP ASSISTANT
Harry? *Hotpants*?

HARRY
One?

VIDEO SHOP ASSISTANT
Two. Not out yet, is it?

HARRY
Nah. *Hotpants One's* in.

GILES
May I place a reservation for *Tex Mex*?

VIDEO SHOP ASSISTANT
No reservations.

GILES
I have to wait two weeks for it to be returned?

VIDEO SHOP ASSISTANT
I 'ope not. You can only take 'em out overnight.

                              GILES
I'll need it for much longer than that.

                    VIDEO SHOP ASSISTANT
Back by six the next day, or you get fined.

                              GILES
But isn't one allowed two weeks at a library?

                    VIDEO SHOP ASSISTANT
Takes two weeks to read a book, doesn't it?

INT. GILES' STUDY – DAY

*Giles sweeps away several volumes of Balzac for Rob to place the
television set on the shelf.*

                              GILES
Tell me, is there any way one can *purchase* video tapes of
films?

                              ROB
You can get just about anything these days. Dead cheap, too.

                              GILES
One can get anything?

                              ROB
Just about. Are you after anything . . . special?

                              GILES
No, no. Just an idle thought.

                              ROB
Like adult material?

                              GILES
Adult?

                              ROB
I can get you loads of that.

GILES

Oh, no, no. Nothing like that. It's just that this is all rather new to me.

ROB

You're telling me! You ready for a run-through?

GILES

I'd better take notes.

The phone rings.

Blasted thing. Hello . . .? Ah, Henry. I can't 'chat' now . . . Of course. I shall see you then. Goodbye, then.

ROB

You need an answerphone. That's what you need. Keeps pests away.

GILES

I don't think it's quite me.

ROB

You wait till you're in the middle of some adult entertainment. You won't want to be disturbed then, I can tell you.

INT. GILES' HOUSE – DUSK

Mrs Barker enters the study where Giles studies the manuals, rehearsing commands on the remote control.

MRS BARKER
(*taking the tray*)
Those things are more trouble than they're worth, if you ask me.

GILES

Mrs Barker, I've been thinking I should start to cope a little more on my own. I'll no longer need you to stay after two o'clock.

MRS BARKER

But . . . what about your dinner?

GILES

I'm quite sure I can manage. And I'd prefer it if you didn't clean in this room. At all.

MRS BARKER

At all?

GILES

There will of course be no reduction in your wage packet. You'll simply have more time to devote to Whitstable, or –

MRS BARKER

But what about the dust?

GILES

Gwen always used to say that the more one dusts, the more dust one makes, Mrs Barker.

She scowls up at the photograph of Gwen, but it has gone.

EXT. GILES' HOUSE – NIGHT

Waiting for her dog to 'do his business', Mrs Reed glances up at the unmistakable flicker of a TV from Giles' windows.

INT. GILES' STUDY – NIGHT

Giles sits in an armchair, the remote control on one arm-rest, the Skid Marks *video box on the other.*

On TV:

EXT. A FARMYARD – DAY

A teenage boy, Rusty, rides a motorbike down a dirt path. Meanwhile Ronnie, in 'swotty' owl-like glasses, checks a trip-wire.

                    PETE

Hey, Prof, this had better work.

                    RONNIE

Cool it, Pete. When have I let you down?

                    PETE

Just make sure you land him in the shit, 'cos that's what he's
gone and done to us.

                    RONNIE
          (*as the motorbike approaches*)
Hey, keep down. Here he comes.

*Rusty is thrown from the bike into a dung-covered haystack. Giles
watches on the edge of his seat.*

                    RUSTY

Shee-it!

                    PETE

Too darned right, bozo. You're in deep shit alright.

                    RONNIE

Man, you know what you are? You're just a skid mark on the
underpants of life!

*Peter and Ronnie go into helpless laughter. Giles fumblingly
pauses the tape, confused. The ambiguity of the remark – and the
film's title – reveals itself. He is disgusted, then capitulates,
breaking into a laugh that shakes his whole frame. He restarts the
tape. Their laughter blends with his.*

EXT. GILES' HOUSE – NIGHT

*A Bernie's Pizza Deliveries moped buzzes to a halt outside. The
boy rings the bell.*

INT. GILES' STUDY – NIGHT

Giles squats on the floor eating the pizza awkwardly with a knife and fork. He hardly takes his eyes off the TV screen.

On TV:

INT. A LOCKER-ROOM – DAY

Rusty keeps a lookout at the door as several other boys stuff socks down their shorts and jockstraps.

> RUSTY
> Hey! Here he comes!

Ronnie enters in glasses and oversized running gear, reading a science book. He looks up. All the boys have comically large bulges under their towels and shorts.

He walks falteringly past them, turns the corner and looks down into his own shorts with a doleful expression.

Giles struggles to freeze-frame it. The image hangs in the air with a fragile, almost abstract beauty. Giles beams with achievement, as if this moment is shared only between the two of them.

INT. GILES' BEDROOM – NIGHT

Giles lies in bed, happily lost in thought. His cigarette smoke swirls in a beam of light from the street lamp.

INT. GILES' STUDY – NIGHT

The time on the video recorder is 4 a.m. It suddenly whirs into Play. Giles, in pyjamas, cannot resist running a scene again.

On TV:

INT. PROF'S BEDROOM – NIGHT

With a towel round his waist, Ronnie steps out of the shower into his bedroom. It is adorned with sports regalia and science charts. He freezes in horror: a girl lies voluptuously across his bed.

GIRL

Don't be scared, honey.

He fumbles for his owl-like glasses.

I'm good with first-timers.

Giles presses the slow-motion button: as Ronnie bolts for the door, the girl lunges across the bed to pull his towel off. The action is fragmented and overlapped; a visual glissando of harp strings.

Giles is transported by this exquisite image, but also by the technological feat that produced it.

INT. THE RESTAURANT – DAY

GILES
(*carefully*)

If one *has* to have a theme, Henry, it would be . . . the discovery of beauty where no one ever thought of looking for it.

HENRY
(*nodding*)

Ah, yes. Familiar territory for you.

GILES

Hardly. I've begun to engage with completely new subject matter. New to me, at least.

HENRY

Splendid! At our time of life, it's good to tackle something new. I was considering golf, actually.

GILES

I could almost say that it's brought me into contact with everything I myself have never been . . .

Henry raises his eyebrows.

But that must be all for the time being, Henry.

54

HENRY

Giles. I'm very intrigued.

GILES

You may find it rather difficult to get 'in touch' with me in the near future.

HENRY

I'm finding it rather difficult now, old chap.

INT. GILES' STUDY – NIGHT

Giles eats pizza with his fingers, gripped by the final scenes of Tex Mex.

On TV:

EXT. SCRUBLAND – DUSK

Ronnie throws himself into a scuffle between youths, to protect two Mexicans.

RONNIE

Hey, cut it out! Are you crazy?

JAKE

Get out the way, Johnny.

RONNIE

This ain't the way, Jake. You heard what Father Bryson said. We gotta learn to live together.

JAKE

No Mexican's gonna take jobs from my folks, Johnny.

RONNIE

They never took any job you ever wanted, Jake, and you know it.

Father Bryson hurries towards them.

JAKE

For the last time, get out my way, Johnny.

As the scuffle continues, Giles' phone rings. An answerphone clicks on!

GILES
(*voice-over*)

This is Giles De'Ath speaking. I am unable to answer the phone at the moment. If your call is extremely urgent, you may leave a brief message after I've finished speaking.

HENRY
(*voice-over*)

Good Lord! . . . Giles!? It's Henry. You have an answerphone? Whatever next? Look, call me as soon as you're back in. What on earth are you up to, you old devil?

On the TV, Jake lunges with a knife. Ronnie staggers a few paces, his grimy T-shirt covered in blood, then sinks into Father Bryson's arms.

RONNIE
(*dying gasps*)

You gone and done it now, Jake.

He looks up at Father Bryson, whose brow is crossed by an unexplainable shaft of light.

FATHER BRYSON
(*with Irish accent*)

Save your breath, my child.

RONNIE

I tried to tell them, Father.

FATHER BRYSON

Hush now. God knows what you say is true, to be sure.

RONNIE

We all gotta live together, like you said. I tried, Father, I . . .

Father Bryson looks up and shakes his head.

JAKE

(*hurling the knife at a tree*)

Johnny! No!

FATHER BRYSON

I promise you won't die in vain, my child. May God rest your soul.

Ronnie utters his last breath. Blood drips from the knife down the tree trunk.

Tears prick Giles' eyes. The pizza's 'extra anchovies' topping drips onto his shirt.

He rewinds the scene to a close-up of Ronnie's vulnerable, trusting face and, eyes closed, tenderly kisses the TV screen. As he makes contact, the shot changes to a close-up of Father Bryson. Opening his eyes, Giles recoils.

INT. GILES' HOUSE – DAY

In the kitchen, Mrs Barker frowns down at a discarded pizza delivery box. Hearing the phone, she proceeds to the study, but the answerphone clicks on. She pauses, then decides to go in.

HENRY

(*voice-over*)

It's Henry again, Giles. Perhaps I need to explain that the idea of an answerphone is that you do eventually reply to the messages, you know.

MRS BARKER

(*picking up the phone*)

Hello . . .? No, he's not . . . I haven't the foggiest. We used to have a nice routine here, but it's all gone to pot.

She tries to pull the locked drawer open.

INT. STEAM BATHS – DAY

Giles sits in towels. Behind him, young men swim naked. Their supple bodies move in a way that seems instinctive and effortless.

INT. GILES' STUDY – DAY

Mrs Barker stands over the desk, wiggling scissors violently in the drawer.

INT. STEAM BATHS – DAY

Giles turns meaningfully but without conviction to watch the men in the pool.

INT. NEWSAGENTS – DAY

Giles looks down at the teen magazines. He raises his eyes dubiously to the top-shelf pornography.

INT. GILES' STUDY – NIGHT

Giles sits in his dressing-gown at the desk, holding the vanished photograph of his late wife. Sighing, he turns it face down and produces a magazine, Hunks, *from the drawer.*

He gingerly opens it to reveal a page of male nudes. He takes cut-outs of Ronnie's head and places them tenderly on the shoulders of the nudes.

Each combination is wrong. The muscular, tattooed, pallid, or hairy bodies affront Ronnie's poise and naivete.

Giles stops, appalled.

He hurls the magazine away, scattering Ronnie's 'heads' into the air like confetti.

GILES

Forgive me, Ronnie.

INT. A UNIVERSITY LECTURE HALL – DAY

A lectern bears the announcement:

> The Constance Winnersch Memorial Lecture:
> GILES De'ATH
> 'The Death of the Future'

GILES
(*clearing his throat*)
It can hardly have escaped your attention that my subject today might also be articulated as the 'Day-aa-th of the Future' . . .

A polite murmur of amusement. Henry is visible amongst the academic throng. He nods to the radio producer. She waves back.

. . . a pun so obvious it could have come from the pen of a journalist. The pun depends of course on the fanciful interplay of meanings, which run the risk of being dangerously ephemeral . . .

Two latecomers clang through the door. Giles glares at them. They hasten back out.

This is nothing less than the abiding nightmare of the writer: to see his work enslaved to the present, rather than preserved as an, ah, 'eternal moment'.

A student taking notes pauses and looks up.

If it's journalists who produce our most transient texts, where then can we look for the greatest degree of permanence?

The audience looks blankly back at him.

I humbly suggest that we lay down our pens and look up at that tantalising palimpsest above us – the cinema screen . . . Isn't it the case that, if one is in the habit of viewing a film more than once, assisted by that technological *aide-memoire* the video player, a remarkable phenomenon presents itself.

59

There is a tremor of surprise in the audience.

We see that what at first appeared merely accidental or unrehearsed becomes, on subsequent viewings, an indelible part of the film's texture: a distant landscape, a blurred face in the crowd, even some banal message on a T-shirt.

The student looks down at his own T-shirt.

The largely unrecognised art of screen-acting therefore lies in the ability of the actor – or actress – to make everything about himself – or herself – seem equally permanent.

The producer leans forward to Henry and makes an amazed gesture. Henry shrugs, amused.

When, thus, an actor is called upon to smile, he must somehow select a smile from a collection, a repertoire, a whole file of smiles, as it were: naive, rueful, sly, sarcastic and so on . . .

We see a montage of Ronnie's smiles from his films. They all look identical.

Giles looks beyond the audience. He smiles slowly. His eyes seem to fill with tears.

EXT./INT. A TAXI – DAY

The lecture has exhausted Giles. He stares out of the window. Henry watches him for some time.

> HENRY
> (*softly*)
> Don't you think you've been overdoing it, old chap . . . ?

Giles does not respond.

We're not as young as we used to be, after all. Maybe you should take a break; go on a trip . . . Do you the world of good.

                              GILES
                          (*disdainfully*)
A trip!

                              HENRY
Yes, I know you think that travel for its own sake is frivolous,
but I must insist that you seriously consider it.

                              GILES
                         (*whimsically*)
A trip?

EXT. A PLANE – DAY

A Jumbo jet cuts distantly across the sky.

                             CAPTAIN
                          (*voice-over*)
It's fifty-two degrees in New York, and we'll be landing in just
a few minutes. If you're seated on the right, there's a fine view
of Long Island at the moment.

EXT. EIGHTH AVE., MANHATTAN – DAY

A yellow cab pulls up at Penn Station.

EXT. A SUBURBAN TRAIN – DAY

*A silver train snakes through woodland, Long Island Railroad
emblazoned on each carriage.*

EXT. CHESTERTON STATION – DAY

*Giles surveys the tiny station's brimming car park with a sense of
achievement. An 'Oyster Bay' taxi pulls up and loads Giles'
luggage.*

INT. A TAXI – DAY

> CAB DRIVER I

A hotel in Chesterton?

> GILES

There must be something, surely.

> CAB DRIVER I

This ain't no resort, mister. Let me take you to Oyster Bay.

> GILES

What about a guest-house, or something of that nature?

> CAB DRIVER I

Well now, there's a motel . . .

> GILES

A motel?

> CAB DRIVER I

On the Expressway.

> GILES

That's quite out of the question.

EXT./INT. A MOTEL – DAY

The motel squats on a busy highway, but the proprietress has delusions of grandeur. She observes Giles with great interest as he registers.

> GILES

The room is quiet?

> MRS ABBOTT

We take a pride in the secluded nature of our accommodation. . . . How long will you be with us?

> GILES

At least a week or two.

MRS ABBOTT

We don't have so many extended-stays here . . . Are you touring Long Island?

GILES

No, no. Not really.

MRS ABBOTT

So Chesterton holds all you desire.
                    (*taking the form*)
A writer! From London, too. Oh my. Well, we're charmed to have you, Mr . . . er . . .

GILES

De-aa-th.

MRS ABBOTT

Well, mister. Anything you want to know about Chesterton, you just ask me.
                    (*pushing the form back to him with a smile*)
You forgot your car license.

INT. MOTEL ROOM – DAY

The room is sparse but neat: bed, table, dresser, a long shelf and huge TV.

Giles searches the telephone directory in vain for Bostock.

He stretches out on the bed. To his consternation there is a ceiling mirror.

EXT. MAIN STREET – DAY

Each store seems tantalisingly to confirm Ronnie's existence: a pizzeria; a Jack Nicholson film poster; Stephen King novels; Reebok trainers; Guns 'N' Roses CDs, which Giles delicately flicks through as if in Ronnie's footsteps.

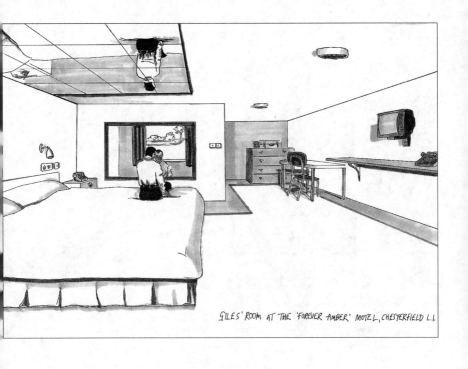

GILES' ROOM AT THE 'FOREVER AMBER' MOTEL, CHESTERFIELD L.I.

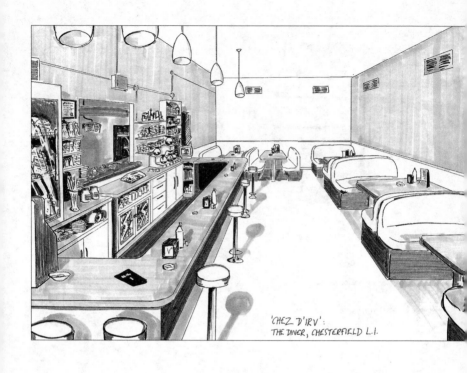

'CHEZ D'IRV':
THE DINER, CHESTERFIELD L.I.

EXT./INT. CHEZ D'IRV – DAY

In a smart but old-fashioned diner festooned with baseball memorabilia, locals have lunch along the counter. The gnarled proprietor emerges from the steamy kitchen and spots Giles in a booth.

IRV

Well, how ya doin'? You're looking just fine today!

GILES

Ah, thank you.

IRV

Anyone taken your order?

GILES

I must admit I'm having a little difficulty understanding the menu. What would you recommend?

IRV

We do a great cheeseburger . . .

GILES

I think not.

IRV

. . . And the best hash browns you ever tasted.

GILES

That rather goes without saying!

IRV

You from England, huh? Ever bumped into a great guy, name of Stan Brighouse?

GILES

I believe not.

IRV

Great guy, Stan. You should look him up. I'm Irv.

GILES
(*shaking his hand*)
Ah! Hence 'Chez d'Irv'?

IRV
You got it! Irving Buckmuller. At your service.

INT./EXT. MOTEL ROOM – NIGHT

Giles lays pressed shirts out on the long wall-shelf and takes his shoes to the door to be left outside for cleaning.

On surveying the windswept parking lot, he changes his mind.

INT. CHEZ D'IRV – DAY

IRV
(*circling an area on Giles' map*)
This here is neat: trees, lawns, bay view. That's where a guy like you should be staying.

GILES
It's secluded?

IRV
(*nodding*)
You'll love it.

GILES
Where the odd celebrity hides out, no doubt?

IRV
You bet! and you know what, they all know Irv's. Everyone knows Irv's.

They look up as a little old lady comes in.

EXT. THE UPLANDS – DAY

In a forested area, Giles passes substantial houses with picket fences, flags on porches, basketball nets over garage doors.

As he exchanges a nod with an elderly jogger (the one seen at the beginning of the film), he spots a Mailman.

> MAILMAN
>
> How're you doing?

> GILES
>
> Good afternoon.

> MAILMAN
>
> That's a great tie.

> GILES
> *(pausing)*
>
> Thank you.

Giles darts a look at the mailbag, which may contain the secret of Ronnie's address.

INT. MOTEL ROOM – NIGHT

Giles sits at the table writing in his notebook. Under *hire detective?* he adds *bribe postman?*

The sound of lovemaking from the next room becomes increasingly evident.

> GILES
> *(seizing the phone)*
>
> This is too much! Mrs Abbott? . . . Is there any possibility of your more, er, 'short-term' guests *not* being given rooms next to mine? . . . I appreciate that, Mrs Abbott, but I also value my own privacy . . . Yes – it is disturbing my work.

He slams the phone down and returns to the table. His map contains so many scribblings it is almost illegible. As the lovemaking reaches its climax, he puts his head in his hands.

> Dear God . . . What on earth am I doing here?

EXT. A PARK – DAY

As skateboarders pass by, Giles is seated on a bench, an incongruously elegant figure in the landscape. He reads the New York Times, *but inside it is concealed a teen magazine.*

> GILES
> (*voice-over, reading*)
> Ronnie plans to make Hollywood his permanent base very soon with a majorly fab home in the Hills . . .

He glances up, perturbed, then falteringly reads on:

> His Dreaminess says he'll be sad to leave Long Island, but feels his career must come first, so now's the time to . . . sell up.

He reads the last line again and smiles.

EXT./INT. A HOUSE FOR SALE – DAY

Giles is shown around a spacious study lined with books, not unlike his London home. The Realtor, a smart professional woman, watches him attentively as he squints at titles on the shelves.

> REALTOR
> Now I can really picture you here.

> GILES
> (*turning slowly*)
> It's not quite . . . I had in mind something a little more . . . youthful?

She blinks at him in surprise.

EXT./INT. ANOTHER HOUSE FOR SALE – DAY

The Realtor opens a door to reveal an overdressed bedroom in daring colours, its walls dominated by black and white art prints of a discreetly homoerotic nature.

> REALTOR

Now isn't this something?

> GILES
> (*a little stunned*)

I, er, yes. It certainly is.

He peers at one of the photographs.

> REALTOR

More . . . youthful?

INT. CHEZ D'IRV – DAY

Giles eats a cheeseburger appreciatively but awkwardly.

> IRV

How's the hunt going?

> GILES

It's taken a promising direction, Irving . . . I must say, these really are delicious.

> IRV

Hey, run that 'bill and check' thing by me again, will you?

> GILES

Of course. Over here, you ask for the check, and pay with a bill. In England we ask for the bill, and pay with a cheque.

> LOU
> (CUSTOMER AT THE COUNTER)

Is that so? I'll be damned!

> IRV

Writer here. From London, England. Likes words.

EXT. THE UPLANDS – DAY

Giles picks up a stray basketball by an empty garage. He light-headedly throws it at the net. To his amusement, it goes through. A police car cruises to a halt beside him.

POLICEMAN

How're you doing today?

GILES

Very well, thank you.

POLICEMAN

You live around here?

GILES

No, no. Or at least not yet. I'm looking at property for sale.

As he fumbles for real-estate leaflets, an unmistakable powder-blue Porsche approaches them.

POLICEMAN

You're moving to Chesterton?

GILES

(*glancing up as the car passes*)

It's a possibili-

POLICEMAN

(*following his gaze*)

Great wheels, huh? . . .

Giles is dumbfounded.

You know, you'd cover a lot more ground in a car.

GILES

(*recovering composure*)

Yes. Yes, I would . . . May I, er, go on my way?

POLICEMAN

Sure. We just like to know what strangers are up to, that's all. You take care now.

He drives off. In his wing-mirror, Giles is visible running after the Porsche.

EXT. A CAR-LOT – DAY

The Porsche is nowhere in sight. Giles leans against a car catching his breath.

> CAR
> (*voiced alarm*)
> You are standing too close to this vehicle.

Giles jolts in surprise and looks around.

> Please move away immediately, or an alarm will be activated.

He looks into the car.

> Move away immediately.

He takes a few steps backwards.

> Thank you. Have a nice day.

INT. MOTEL ROOM – NIGHT

Giles bathes his feet in the shower. On the shelf beside real-estate leaflets sits an old typewriter with a typed note: 'For your work . . .'

The phone rings. Giles hobbles over.

> GILES
> Hello . . .? Ah, Mrs Abbott. A typewriter has appeared in my room . . . How very thoughtful . . . Cocktails? I'm afraid not. I have to be up at the crack of dawn.

EXT. THE UPLANDS – DAY

Garage doors open to reveal every car but a Porsche; of all colours but powder blue.

> GILES
> (*limping slightly*)
> Good morning.

MAILMAN

How're you doing? . . . What happened to your foot?

GILES

Oh, just a blister or two.

MAILMAN

You take it easy now.

He returns to his jeep, greeting a dog as it shakes itself on the grass verge.

Hey, Strider, you get back home!

Giles stops dead and mouths 'Strider'. As the jeep moves off, he is visible in its wing-mirror pursuing the dog up the road. As it turns into Ronnie's house, Giles stops by its 'For Sale' sign and hungrily surveys the windows. The dog pricks up its ears.

GILES

Strider?

Strider barks. Giles beats a hasty retreat.

INT. CHEZ D'IRV – DAY

IRV

Lassie? Rin Tin Tin?

LOU

I had one called Tiffy.

IRV

That's a pansy name, Lou. Who calls their dog Tiffy?

LOU

Lived to be fifteen, Tiffy.

CUSTOMER I

There's a lot of Caesars about.

CUSTOMER 2

What about Spot?

IRV

That's it! That's what everyone calls their dog. Spot.

GILES

What if the dog has no spots?

IRV

Then they call it Patch, I guess. You wanna dog, Giles?

GILES

Oh, no! I've heard some unusual names, that's all . . . Is . . .
Strider common?

IRV

I ain't heard that one. Anyone heard of Strider?

CUSTOMER 1

Sure. Strider, Caesar. They're all a damn nuisance.

LOU

Hey! You never knew Tiffy.

EXT./INT. RONNIE'S HOUSE – DAY

*The Realtor's car sits outside. She shows Giles the neat, sparse,
rather feminine living room.*

GILES
(*despondently*)

I feel rather guilty taking up so much of your time.

REALTOR

Not at all. It's a pleasure to have such a discerning client . . .

*He looks in vain once more for any trace of Ronnie as she leads
him into the luxurious kitchen.*

REALTOR
(*flirtatiously*)
We call this an 'island counter'. I guess you'd call it something
else in England?

GILES
Yes, we probably would.

The phone rings.

ANSWERPHONE
(*Audrey's voice-over*)
Hi, we're not in. Leave a message.

REALTOR
Do you cook?

GILES
No. No, I don't.

ANSWERPHONE
(*woman's voice-over*)
Audrey, it's your mother. Do you know when you're leaving
yet? You know how your father worries . . .

The Realtor smiles and starts to lead him out.

. . . He wants you both here for Thanksgiving, by the way.
Call me. Oh, and love to Ronnie.

Giles stops dead and closes his eyes in disbelief.

REALTOR
(*from the hall*)
I've got one or two new places to show you . . . What you'd
call 'bachelor pads'?

*Giles darts back into the living room. She finds him gazing around
voraciously. Everything now tingles with significance for him.*

You're sure you don't see any potential here?

GILES
(*breathless*)
Quite sure! . . . Maybe . . . just to be *certain* . . . I could see
upstairs again?

INT. MOTEL ROOM – NIGHT

*Giles lies on the bed in a blissful state. His reflection in the ceiling
mirror gives way to fantasy:*

INT. RONNIE'S KITCHEN – DAY

Ronnie in Hotpants *pizza-parlor outfit takes a pizza from the oven
and wipes sweat from his brow.*

INT. RONNIE'S LIVING ROOM – DAY

Bespectacled as Skid Marks' *Prof, Ronnie lounges on the floor
with Pete, manipulating a video game with great skill.*

INT. RONNIE'S BEDROOM – DAY

*Father Bryson lays out Ronnie's limp body in his bloodstained
outfit from* Tex Mex.

EXT. RONNIE'S HOUSE – DAY

*Dissolves establish that Giles walks once, twice, three times past
the house, always checking it discreetly for signs of life.*

*The fourth time, the garage door suddenly grunts into action. Giles
is rooted to the spot.*

*Strider ambles out joyfully, but freezes as he detects the intruder.
They look at each other for a few seconds before he flies barking
down the drive towards Giles.*

*Giles plunges into woodland beside the house as Audrey follows
the dog out.*

                              AUDREY
Strider? Strider! What is it, boy? . . . It's just a squirrel, you
idiot.

She leads him back by the collar.

        Come on. In. I can't take you to the supermarket. Jesus!

*A car starts. She drives the Porsche out of the garage. Giles catches
sight of her – a stylish woman a few years older than Ronnie.*

*He tumbles out of the undergrowth, brushing himself down. A
woman driving by slows down to stare.*

*He runs off in pursuit of the Porsche, overtaking the jogger, who
slows to a halt in surprise.*

EXT. THE UPLANDS – DAY

*On a busier road, Giles runs in front of an 'Oyster Bay' cab,
waving his arms.*

                              GILES
It's an emergency.

                          CAB DRIVER 2
You need a hospital?

                              GILES
The nearest supermarket.

INT. SUPERMARKET – DAY

*Giles stalks the aisles, taking groceries at random from the shelves.
He finally locates Audrey and, bracing himself, stages an almighty
crash between their carts.*

                              AUDREY
Hey! What's the idea?

                              GILES
I'm dreadfully sorry. I hope nothing's broken?

                               81

AUDREY

I guess not.

GILES

We don't have things of this size in England. Very tricky to control.

AUDREY
(*moving off*)

That's OK. Take it easy.

GILES
(*fumbling for words*)

Haven't we met?

AUDREY
(*not stopping*)

I don't think so.

GILES

No! I've seen your photographs!

She heaves a sigh.

You're a film star?

AUDREY

Would you mind just leaving me alone?

GILES

Of course! You're engaged to Abigail's idol!

AUDREY
(*stopping angrily*)

I could really do without this.

GILES
(*hurriedly*)

My godchild, Abigail, has a huge crush on a very promising young actor: 'Ronnie Bostock', isn't it? You made a very handsome couple.

                    AUDREY
              (*intrigued but cautious*)
        You saw our picture in England?

INT. THE SUPERMARKET TILL – DAY

                    AUDREY
        What kind of books do you write?

                     GILES
        Oh, I'm hardly a household name over here.

                    AUDREY
        Are you working on one now?

                     GILES
        If I'm inspired by the 'soothing rustle' of the Long Island surf;
        as your Walt Whitman put it.

                    AUDREY
        I hope you have a great time.

                     GILES
        Are you over for a while?

                    AUDREY
        Excuse me?

                     GILES
        From Hollywood.

                    AUDREY
        We live here.

                     GILES
        Really?

                    AUDREY
        Actually we're moving out west real soon, but all my contacts
        are here in the city. I'm a model.

                        83

GILES

I can see why.

AUDREY

Ron's in LA right now.

GILES

Oh, is he?

AUDREY

I just can't believe he's so big in England. I never knew that.

INT./EXT. AUDREY'S CAR – DAY

GILES
(clutching his groceries)
It's extremely kind of you.

AUDREY

This isn't Manhattan, you know. You can't just hail a cab.
They don't stop.

GILES

Indeed.

AUDREY

You've got a lot of groceries for someone staying at a motel.

GILES

I've always been rather vague about domestic arrangements,
but I wanted to find out how Americans shop – what you eat
and so on. I can in fact heartily recommend the cheeseburgers
at 'Chez d'Irv'.

AUDREY

God. You've been to that dive?

GILES

Maybe you could recommend somewhere superior?

84

                              AUDREY
There are some great seafood places up the coast, but you
gotta drive there.

                              GILES
Well, let me invite you to lunch.

                              AUDREY
Oh, I couldn't. Really.

                              GILES
To thank you for your kindness.

                              AUDREY
I don't think so.

                              GILES
Please don't misunderstand. My intentions are strictly
honourable.

                              AUDREY
                             (*smiling*)
I don't know. It would be great to hear about Europe . . . but
I'm just so busy . . .

INT. SEAFOOD RESTAURANT – DAY

Giles and Audrey are in animated conversation. Giles lights a
cigarette. A waiter appears immediately, remonstrates, and takes it
from him. Audrey is amused.

INT. RONNIE'S LIVING ROOM – DAY

Audrey is conducting Giles through her portfolio. There is a slight
attraction between them.

                              GILES
Very impressive. You're both very talented, my dear.

                              AUDREY
Thanks.

RONNIE + AUDREY'S LIVING ROOM.

GILES

It must be challenging, looking your best for the camera day in, day out?

AUDREY

Oh, I've been doing it since I was in diapers.

GILES
(*confused*)

Diapers?

He sips an imposing cappuccino.

AUDREY

It's de-caff. I hope that's OK?

GILES

One would never guess there was anything missing.

He glances serenely around the room.

You give Ronnie tips, no doubt?

AUDREY

Tips?

GILES

Doesn't he have to do photographs, for the fan magazines?

AUDREY

Oh, photoshoots! Tell me about it. He hates them.

GILES

He seems rather good at it?

AUDREY

Oh, sure. It's just – he thinks you can't be a teen idol if you're gonna be a serious actor.

GILES

Oh, does he?

AUDREY

It's crazy. I mean, he's been so lucky. Most of the actors I know wait tables . . .

Pause.

GILES

Why would they do that?

AUDREY
(*smiling*)

I can't wait to tell him I've met a famous British writer who thinks he's got the look of a young . . . Olivier, was it?

GILES
(*cautiously*)

A little.

AUDREY

I should be writing this down. Hey, maybe you could do a script for him, or something?

GILES

Well, I don't exactly write for the 'youth market', Audrey.

AUDREY

That's great! He's *so* sick of playing dumb kids.

The phone rings in the kitchen. Audrey stands up then sits down again.

It's OK. The machine's on.

ANSWERPHONE
(*Audrey's voice-over*)

Hi, we're not in. Leave a message.

ANSWERPHONE
(*Ronnie's voice-over*)

Hey, babe. I guess you're out . . . Again . . .

88

> AUDREY

It's Ron.

Giles' features flicker. A tremor of excitement runs through him as he listens to Ronnie 'live'. His voice sounds deeper than on screen.

> ANSWERPHONE
> (*Ronnie's voice-over*)

Hey, you better not be having a good time without me. Things are pretty cool here. Love ya.

> AUDREY
> (*smiling*)

I'll call him later . . . Oh, Giles, I forgot. You can smoke here if you want. We don't, but . . . Giles . . . ? Are you OK?

> GILES
> (*weakly*)

Would you excuse me, my dear?

INT. RONNIE'S BATHROOM – DAY

Giles splashes water on his face and looks at his reflection in the mirrored cupboard.

> GILES

Dear God. This is ridiculous.

He cannot resist opening the cupboard. From a shelf that is clearly Ronnie's, he takes a toothbrush and rubs his thumb along it.

INT. RONNIE'S BEDROOM – DAY

The sound of Audrey on the phone filters upstairs. By the ominously large bed, Giles slides open a drawer. Boxer shorts patterned with cartoon characters sit jauntily on top.

INT. THE SPARE ROOM – DAY

Among packing boxes and juvenilia sits Ronnie's guitar. Giles runs his hand across its strings. It makes an untuned clang.

INT. RONNIE'S STAIRCASE – DAY

Giles comes downstairs as Audrey continues her call.

> AUDREY
> (*quietly*)
> It's, like, just amazing. He's seen all your stuff, and he says that in Europe they really, you know, rate you. You'd just love him. He's so English you wouldn't believe it . . .

Giles pauses on the stairs as she laughs.

> Screw you! Are you crazy? He's old enough to be my father! . . .

Strider appears at the bottom of the stairs and bares his teeth.

> GILES
> (*clearing his throat*)
> Er, Audrey!

> AUDREY
> Listen, I gotta go . . . Love you, too. Bye now.
> (*appearing in the hallway*)
> Strider! I'm sorry, Giles. I've never seen him like this.

EXT. AUDREY'S CAR – NIGHT

Audrey drives Giles back to the motel.

> GILES
> So Ronnie will be back soon?

> AUDREY
> Uh huh.

GILES

Would you give him my regards?

AUDREY

Sure.

GILES

Do tell him that I'll be following his career with great interest.

AUDREY

Maybe *you* should tell him . . .

Giles holds his breath.

I'd like him to meet you . . .

Giles waits an eternity.

I guess you're busy, though? With your writing?

GILES

Well, I am, but . . .

AUDREY

Oh, I dunno. We're really busy, too. And he can get kind of shy . . . I dunno. Maybe I'll call you.

Giles closes his eyes with relief.

EXT. MOTEL RECEPTION – NIGHT

Mrs Abbott watches in amazement as Giles clambers out of the shiny Porsche.

INT. MOTEL ROOM – DAY

Cans and packets from the supermarket are laid out neatly along the shelf.

Giles lies in bed, elated. We hear Ronnie's answerphone message again, as Giles replays it in his mind.

INT. MOTEL RECEPTION – DAY

> MRS ABBOTT

A tin opener!

> GILES

I'd be most grateful.

> MRS ABBOTT

You mean for opening cans?

> GILES

Yes.

> MRS ABBOTT
> (*huffily*)

A can opener. There's a general store just by the station.

> GILES

I really can't leave at the moment, even for an hour.

> MRS ABBOTT

You're writing?

> GILES

I'm . . . writing, yes.

> MRS ABBOTT

Ah. Maybe I can find one.

> GILES

I'd be most grateful.

INT. MOTEL ROOM – NIGHT

A can opener lies on the shelf. Most of the groceries have been eaten.

Dissolves establish Giles watching TV; pacing the room; re-positioning the phone; stretching out on the bed; sitting at the table, pen poised but unable to write. He suddenly becomes aware of the ticking of his watch.

EXT./INT. MOTEL ROOM – DAY

Unshaven and dishevelled, Giles glances out of the window and sees Mrs Abbott passing by. He dutifully pretends to type. She smiles as she hears his clatter on the keys.

INT. MOTEL ROOM – NIGHT

Fully dressed, Giles lies on the bed curled around the phone. His reflection in the ceiling mirror gives way to:

INT. RONNIE'S BATHROOM – DAY

Wearing the cartoon boxer shorts, Ronnie caresses his famous front teeth with the toothbrush. Audrey appears and hugs him.

INT. RONNIE'S BEDROOM – NIGHT

Ronnie lowers his head to kiss Audrey. They are making love on the big, wide bed.

INT. RONNIE'S LIVING ROOM – NIGHT

Ronnie plays his guitar, wearing the cartoon boxer shorts.

INT. MOTEL ROOM – DAY

The guitar strumming gradually and deliciously becomes the sound of the phone ringing. Giles wakes with a start and stares down at it, as if it were a call to arms.

EXT. MAIN STREET – DAY

Giles visits a barber's and a florist's.

INT. MOTEL ROOM – DAY

Six ties are laid out across the bed. Giles' hand tenderly passes along them, assessing their merits. He appears deep in thought, as if he is preparing for a speech.

EXT. THE HOTEL – DAY

Mrs Abbott watches Audrey drive Giles away. He nods to her, as if he will never return.

EXT. THE BEACH – DAY

The beach is deserted except for Ronnie, a tiny figure on the horizon. Strider wanders jubilantly around him.

Ronnie stares out to sea, his trousers rolled up to his knee, his trainers dangling over a shoulder. One hand rests rakishly on a hip. It is a moment of beautiful contemplation for Giles.

Ronnie glances over his shoulder and waves. As he strolls towards Giles and Audrey, he appears increasingly different from his film appearances. He looks older, with hair long enough to be forced into a ponytail and a careless combination of clothes.

As he comes still closer, facial hair is visible; more than stubble but not quite enough to constitute a fashionable goatee.

Giles squints against the setting sun. His look of absolute pleasure gives way to doubt, then apprehension, then intrigue, as to whether this is indeed he.

From a great distance, we see Ronnie join Giles and Audrey, a tiny grouping of human complication in the epic landscape.

In extreme close-up, they shake hands against the distant crashing of waves.

EXT. RONNIE'S HOUSE – DUSK

Audrey arranges Giles' flowers in the kitchen as a police car sweeps up the drive. The door bell rings.

AUDREY
Can you get that, honey?

INT. RONNIE'S LIVING ROOM – DUSK

The room is more cluttered than before, with strewn CDs, magazines and script pages. Giles perches on one of the couches; edgy, uncertain.

> AUDREY
> (*bringing his flowers in*)
These are lovely, Giles!

She sits beside him and drops her voice.

So what do you think? Of Ronnie?

> GILES

Oh, he seems very pleasant . . . A little different from what I'd expected, perhaps . . .

> AUDREY

OK. He may not show it, right, but he really wants to hear what you told me – about his potential?

> GILES

Oh, really?

> AUDREY

Really. He's been kind of low since he got back. If you could find some way of telling him what you think of him, well, I'd really appreciate it.

Giles is rather startled by the request. They hear the front door shut.

> RONNIE
> (*from the hallway*)
Well, whaddaya know! . . . Anyone need a beer in there?

> AUDREY

Who was it, honey?

> RONNIE
> (*from the kitchen*)

The cops! They're keeping an eye on the place. A neighbour saw some weirdo hanging about.

> AUDREY

Oh, yeah. I forgot to tell you.

She notices Giles frown, perturbed.

It's nothing, really, Giles . . .

She takes his glass to the door.

I'll get you another Scotch . . . Or we've got bourbon?

> RONNIE
> (*appearing at the door*)

We have?

> GILES

Scotch is fine.

Ronnie nuzzles up behind her, holding his can of beer to her lips – a clumsy gesture of affection that is painful to Giles. Audrey brushes Ronnie gently away.

> RONNIE

I don't know how you can drink that stuff.

He flops down on the other couch facing Giles and takes a swig. Giles watches him closely, intrigued rather than beguiled. Ronnie looks up and smiles a little shyly.

So. Giles . . . Aud's told me a lot about you. You seem like a really interesting kind of a guy . . .

Giles smiles enigmatically.

How do you like Long Island?

> GILES

Very much.

RONNIE

We like it. Aud's from round here.

Audrey returns with Giles' drink.

AUDREY

You have to see the Hamptons, Giles. Some of the beach-houses there. Jeez. They'll be closed up now but they're fabulous.

RONNIE

There's better stuff in California; kind of Spanish.

AUDREY

Woody Allen's got one. They shot one of his movies there . . . Which one was it, Ron?

RONNIE

I dunno.

AUDREY

We've not seen it, anyways.

GILES

The house, or the film?

AUDREY

Oh, both.

A timer rings in the kitchen. She rises to leave the room.

It's nothing special, I'm afraid. I've got a shoot tomorrow, so it's just been crazy today.

Pause.

RONNIE

You want ice in that?

GILES

No, no. It's fine.

Pause.

People do seem to like ice over here. And lettuce.

RONNIE

You don't like lettuce?

GILES

Not with everything . . .

Pause.

I understand you've been in Los Angeles?

RONNIE

Right.

GILES

A new project?

RONNIE

Well, it's kind of not that new. But the part's bigger.

GILES

Than . . .

RONNIE

The last one. It's a sequel.

GILES

Oh, is it?

AUDREY
(*looking at Giles significantly*)
It's *Hotpants College III*, Giles. Open the wine, will you,
honey?

RONNIE

Yeah, well. It's a bigger part, and they had to pay for it . . .
We're gonna be based over there soon.

He fumbles with the corkscrew.

GILES

Would you like me to do that?

Ronnie looks up at him gratefully.

INT. RONNIE'S DINING ROOM – NIGHT

The mood has changed. Giles is in absolute control, but speaks with a real passion. Ronnie, a little drunk, listens intensely.

RONNIE
(reverently)

Shakespeare?

GILES

Oh, yes. His plays are full of it.

RONNIE
(slowly)

You're saying Shakespeare would be doing things like *Hotpants* now?

GILES

All I'm saying, Ronnie, is that he used bawdy humour – to please the mob in the pit.

RONNIE

I never knew that.

GILES

But he was able to elevate his material beyond such limitations, as have you . . .

He confidently takes a sip of wine.

I'm not talking about 'good acting' as if it were merely, say, 'good cooking' – By the way, the pot roast was delicious, Audrey . . .

AUDREY

Thanks!

GILES

I'm talking about a type of acting that is purely instinctive.

You see, Ronnie, you have something that gives even the most casual look or gesture a real intensity.

> RONNIE

Yeah?

> GILES

Oh, yes. I do know about these things. It was no surprise to me to hear that you were rescued at an early age from the hell of advertising –

> (*To Audrey*)

No offense, my dear . . .

She smiles weakly.

> . . . and propelled into the more challenging world of the sitcom.

Ronnie nods slowly.

> It's obvious that some astute producer saw what I saw, when Abigail persuaded me to let her see *Hotpants College II*.

> RONNIE

But I got that part 'cos I look a bit like the guy that played Mikey in the original.

> GILES

But didn't you entirely re-invent the character? With a mere string of lines, didn't you make 'Mikey' the focus of the entire story?

> RONNIE

Well, I don't know; I wouldn't say that . . .

He sneaks a smile at Audrey.

> GILES

And as for your fate in the pizza parlor – the plastic tomato and so on. This may sound absurd, but my point of reference would be Wallis' painting of the tragic young writer Chatterton, which hangs in the Tate Gallery.

                              AUDREY
I'd really like to see that.

                              RONNIE
But we've watched *Hotpants* with, like, kids, and . . . they
don't see all that.

                              GILES
Of course not.

                              RONNIE
But it's made for them.

                              GILES
They're the rabble in the pit.

                              RONNIE
They just laugh at the dirty stuff.

                              AUDREY
We saw *Hotpants* at this drive-in that used to be here. Ron
kept his sunglasses on the whole time.

                              RONNIE
Have you seen *Tex Mex*?

                              GILES
I have indeed – more than once.

                              RONNIE
It really killed me when it flopped.

                              GILES
                        (*authoritatively*)
Ah, yes. I'm afraid it suffered the same fate in Europe.

                              RONNIE
It kind of had this real *message*. I really believed in that movie.

                              GILES
It's a great shame really. In Europe, we have a much stronger
tradition of work with what you call a *message*. That is, after

all, why I've been persuaded to write my first screenplay.

Ronnie's eyes flicker with interest.

No. If *Tex Mex* had been German, about the plight of exploited 'gastarbeiters', it would have met with far greater success.

AUDREY
They have Mexicans in Germany?

Pause.

GILES
It would probably have made less money than *Hotpants*, but in Europe we're not interested in that kind of success – not when, with the right casting, a film can change the way people think.

He drains his glass.

And that, Ronnie, is why I write. And that's also why you act – although you may not yet know it.

Ronnie is reeling. Every word is precious to him. The silence is suddenly fractured.

AUDREY
Cappuccino, Giles?

RONNIE
(*belligerently*)
Jesus! Can't your cappuccino wait?

She goes defiantly into the kitchen.

Women!

Giles smiles complicitly.

INT. RONNIE'S LIVING ROOM – NIGHT

RONNIE
You married or something?

GILES

I was. My wife died unexpectedly some years ago.

RONNIE

That's really tough; I'm sorry. Any kids?

GILES

No, no. My wife was rather older than myself.

RONNIE
(*proudly*)

Like me and Aud!

GILES
(*amused*)

Indeed.

RONNIE

So, what's this script?

GILES

Script?

RONNIE

You're working on a screenplay?

GILES
(*airily*)

Oh, that. Yes.

RONNIE

So what's it about?

GILES

Oh, I . . . I really couldn't subject you to work in progress.

RONNIE

Why not?

GILES

You'd find it rather boring.

RONNIE

No way. I'm really interested.

GILES

(*playfully*)

And then there's the risk of copyright infringement.

RONNIE

But we're old friends, Giles.

Giles glances at the kitchen.

GILES

Well . . .

RONNIE

Please? Coffee always takes her for ever.

GILES

Indeed.

RONNIE

So . . .

GILES

(*confidentially*)

Well . . . It concerns a young man, Ronnie, about your age I suppose. He's a deaf-mute, brought up in complete isolation. The only human contact he has is with the television. And so he's exposed to rather excessive and unrealistic types of behaviour.

RONNIE

He never speaks?

GILES

He cannot speak.

RONNIE

Wow.

I'm determined that the audience *share* his subjective state rather than merely pity him. That would be awful –

RONNIE
(*nodding intensely*)

So what happens?

GILES

Well, he develops a keen intelligence from this rather unlikely source. Understandably enough, he yearns to enter the 'real world', so he surrenders himself to the most irrational desire known to mankind . . . Maybe you can guess what that is?

Ronnie shakes his head, spellbound.

It's the desire to fall in love, Ronnie. Since he's seen such a thing on the television every day, it becomes his quest, so to speak. And every tale, whether it be *Richard the Third* or *Hotpants College the Third*, centres upon a quest . . .

Ronnie nods slowly.

As in my other work, it will inevitably end with a sacrifice. The French in particular seem to like such a thing. I suspect it's not one for the drive-ins, though.

Audrey brings the coffee in.

Ah, thank you, my dear. De-caff, no doubt?

AUDREY

Uh huh.

RONNIE

Thanks, babe.

She returns sulkily to the kitchen.

(*To Giles*)

It's brilliant.

GILES

Oh, I don't think so. Not yet, at least.

RONNIE

Kind of arty, I guess . . .

GILES

Oh dear. Is that bad?

RONNIE

No way . . . It's just . . . I never heard a storyline like that. Never. It's blown me away.

GILES

That's very kind of you.

RONNIE

You seen *Birdy*?

GILES

Birdy?

RONNIE

Yeah. Sounds a bit like *Birdy*. Alan Parker. I've met him. He's from England too . . .

Giles glances round as he hears a soft ringing tone.

It's just a fax.

Paper starts to purr through the machine.

More rewrites, I guess.

GILES
(*intrigued*)

Oh, really?

Audrey returns with a saucer.

AUDREY

You can smoke, Giles.

RONNIE

You smoke? Bad habit, man.

He dangles an arm over Audrey's shoulder: an apology. His shirt has come undone, revealing the mole on the left of his neck. Giles notices this mark of authentication.

AUDREY
(sulkily)
We'd never have met if he didn't.

RONNIE

Huh?

AUDREY

Giles chose to stay in Chesterton because he smokes Chesterton's!

RONNIE

Yeah? Wow.

AUDREY

Giles? You know what you were saying about being a writer and wanting new experiences and all? . . . Oh, I don't know. Maybe it's not such a good idea.

RONNIE
(rubbing her cheek)
Come on, babe. Tell us.

AUDREY

I was just thinking. I got a shoot in the city tomorrow, and I just thought maybe you'd like to come?

RONNIE
(removing his arm)
God! They're so boring.

AUDREY

No necessarily. Not if you haven't been on one.

RONNIE

Well, *I'm* not coming.

AUDREY

I'm not asking *you*.

RONNIE

They're *totally* boring, Giles.

GILES

Wouldn't I be in the way?

AUDREY

I'd love you to come. I'm sure you'd get some great ideas.

RONNIE

I've got a better idea, Giles. I'll show you the Hamptons.

AUDREY

You don't like the Hamptons.

RONNIE

I do out of season. What d'you say, Giles?

GILES

Well, I . . . Such a choice! One couldn't, er, do both?

RONNIE

No way.

Pause.

Tell you what. If the weather's OK, we go to the coast. If it's raining, you go to the city with Miss Supermodel.

GILES

Well, that does sound fair.

RONNIE

OK, babe?

EXT./INT. MOTEL ROOM – NIGHT

An 'Oyster Bay' cab leaves the motel. In his room, Giles flips TV channels madly.

On screen:

INT. TV STUDIO – NIGHT

WEATHERMAN

So, things look good for Washington and Baltimore tomorrow. It's a different story in New York. Just look at those clouds gobbling up Manhattan. They're sure to bring rain tomorrow and plenty of it. Over in Long Island, it's gonna be even worse, with both coasts pulling in that low pressure.

INT./EXT. MOTEL ROOM – DAY

Giles staggers from his bed to the window, aware of the ominous sound of rain. He pulls open the curtains to reveal blazing sunshine and Mrs Abbott hosing a pathetic flower-bed.

EXT. LONG ISLAND MONTAGE – DAY

Ronnie drives Giles past a beautiful stretch of water.

They drive through East Hampton's smart and village-like main street, then down tree-lined lanes with imposing mansions.

On a beach of white sand and surf, Ronnie throws a stone along the surface of the water. To his disapproval, Giles lights a cigarette with difficulty in the breeze.

*At a gas station, two teenage girls approach Ronnie. Giles watches
with intrigue as he signs an autograph and kisses them. He returns
to the car, shrugging sheepishly. He hands Giles a can of Pepsi,
which Giles finds unexpectedly pleasant.*

*The car pulls up in front of a picturesque coastal vista, a place
where lovers often stop. Ronnie is clean-shaven and dressed more
smartly than before. He puts sunglasses on and offers a pair to
Giles, who eventually accepts, despite their youthful style. The car
sits beside an empty billboard which strangely resembles a cinema
screen. On it we see an almost imperceptible image of Ronnie from
one of his films.*

*The car negotiates a series of gentle hills, catching the first rays of
sunset.*

INT. MOTEL RECEPTION – DUSK

> GILES
>
> My dear Mrs Abbott!

> MRS ABBOTT
>
> What's wrong now?

> GILES
>
> Good evening, good evening, good evening.

> MRS ABBOTT
>
> The sun really shone for you today.

> GILES
>
> It certainly did. Everything is absolutely perfect, and I am in
> overwhelming need of a cocktail with my charming hostess. If
> the offer still stands, of course.

> MRS ABBOTT
>
> You got something to celebrate?

> GILES
>
> I have indeed.

MRS ABBOTT
You got your work done!

GILES
My work is moving at a pace I can hardly keep up with, and after such a long period of, er, exile from humanity, I would value your company, Mrs Abbott.

MRS ABBOTT
Shirley.

GILES
Shirley.

INT. RONNIE'S HOUSE – DUSK

Audrey lounges on the couch reading a magazine. She hears Ronnie come in.

RONNIE
(*from the door*)
Hey, babe. Good day? Bad day?

AUDREY
It was fine.

RONNIE
(*from the kitchen*)
Giles and I hung out all day. He's coming over tomorrow. We're gonna work on the new *Hotpants*.

AUDREY
Am I invited?

Ronnie walks in with a beer. His hair is cut short, closer to how it appeared in the films.

RONNIE
Sure.

                         AUDREY
What happened to your hair!?

                         RONNIE
I had it cut, that's what.

                         AUDREY
Why'd you have it cut?

                         RONNIE
I dunno.

                         AUDREY
I kind of liked it long.

                         RONNIE
                    (*shrugging*)
It's got to be short for the part, so . . . D'you wanna watch the
game at Steve's tonight?

She looks at him quizzically.

EXT. MOTEL FORECOURT – NIGHT

Giles, slightly drunk, wobbles towards his room, singing the Skid
Marks *theme tune under his breath.*

                         GILES
Skid marks . . . Ooh yeah, skid marks, baby . . . Sure gonna
burn some rubber tonite!

INT. MOTEL ROOM – NIGHT

*Giles lies in bed, deeply contented. We travel in to his eye, which
gives way to:*

INT. STUDIO – DAY

*Ronnie, as Giles' deaf-mute character, crouches against a white
wall, illuminated by the flicker from a TV set. He copies gestures
and facial expressions from it.*

INT. RONNIE'S BEDROOM – NIGHT

Pull out of Ronnie's eye to reveal that Audrey is asleep, but Ronnie lies awake, fantasising about the same scene as Giles.

INT. DAY RONNIE'S LIVING ROOM – DAY

On the back terrace, Giles tests Ronnie on lines from the Hotpants *script.*

GILES
Hey, dude. How's it hanging?

RONNIE
It's cool.

GILES
Hey, man, I'm real sorry about your mother. Life's a bitch, huh?

RONNIE
I guess. You know something, Brad? I just wish I could've made things easier for her.

GILES
Yeah?

RONNIE
Seems like she was always working and stuff. There was never any time to get to know her.

GILES
Hey, man. Don't grief-out on me!

RONNIE
Sorry, Brad. It's just, I've been feeling a bit lonesome, you know?

GILES
Hey! You're a college boy now. All those babes don't want you to feel lonesome!

RONNIE

Oh, sure! Like I'm Mr Popular.

Audrey approaches with a tray of drinks and a mobile phone.

GILES

Well I'm gonna make you Mr Popular, and that's a promise.

He lowers the script and smiles.

Hmm. A poignant little scene.

RONNIE

It's to set up the storyline. The college girls try and mother me, but I fall for a teacher whose husband has to be exposed as a racist bigot.

GILES

Hmm. Something of a *message* there?

RONNIE

It's the usual stuff.

Giles leafs through the script.

GILES

Do you have the chance to deliver a eulogy to your mother?

RONNIE

No way. It would hold up the action.

GILES

Are you allowed to improvise?

RONNIE

They get real nervous about wasting time.

GILES
(*throwing up his hands*)

What can I say?

AUDREY

You guys need a break.

GILES
(*taking a drink*)
Thank you, Audrey.

RONNIE
Where've you been hiding out?

AUDREY
I was talking to our neighbour. Is that OK? . . .

GILES
Is this one of those phones that don't have to be plugged in?

They both smile. He handles it cautiously.

Remarkable, really, isn't it?

AUDREY
Hey, I've had a great idea! Giles, why don't we call your
godchild in England?

GILES
I'm sorry?

He hurriedly puts the phone down.

AUDREY
Abigail, wasn't it? You could call her and tell her you're sitting
here with Ronnie Bostock, and Ron could say hi to her. I
know she'd just die!

GILES
(*stunned*)
I'm afraid it's the middle of the night in England.

AUDREY
They're only five hours ahead.

They all look at the mobile phone.

RONNIE
That's the dumbest thing I ever, ever, ever, ever heard. What

am I going to say to some kid? Jesus! I'm sorry, Giles . . .
Jesus, Aud!

He looks at her contemptuously, but she is watching Giles closely.

EXT./INT. MOTEL ROOM – NIGHT

The sound of hesitant, one-finger typing leaks from Giles' room.

Inside, with the Hotpants *script open on the desk, he types an
additional scene:*

Ronnie is at his mother's grave.

> RONNIE
> I'd like to say a few words by Walt Whitman, if that's OK
> with everyone . . .

We see how Giles imagines it:

EXT. GRAVEYARD – DAY

Ronnie dressed as Mikey in Hotpants *at his mother's grave,
surrounded by cast members.*

> RONNIE
> I'd like to say a few words by Walt Whitman, if that's OK
> with everyone . . .

He pulls out a crumpled piece of paper.

> 'Now finale to the shore,
> Now land and life finale and farewell.
> The untold want by life and land never granted,
> Now voyager sail thou forth to seek and find.'

*He replaces his baseball cap, his face wet with tears. The cast
members all turn and look at each other in complete confusion.*

*Giles drops out of this reverie and starts to chuckle, shaking his
head.*

EXT./INT. MOTEL ROOM – DAY

The Porsche slinks past the motel reception.

Giles hears its distinctive sound, checks his appearance and throws open the door.

> AUDREY
>
> Hi, Giles.

> GILES
>
> Audrey! No aerobics this morning?

EXT. AUDREY'S CAR – DAY

Audrey drives recklessly through a Stop sign. An approaching car hoots at her.

EXT. A PARK – DAY

Giles breathes a sigh of relief as they come to a halt near an impromptu baseball game.

> GILES
>
> I thought you were trying to kill us both, my dear.

> AUDREY
>
> I'm sorry. I didn't get much sleep.

Giles starts to clamber out of the car.

> AUDREY
> (*sharply*)
>
> Hold it. Ron's busy right now.

Giles searches the distant group for him.

> GILES
>
> I suspect you'll have to explain the rules to me.

> AUDREY
>
> OK. You gotta hit the ball and run round the bases to home.

GILES

Ah. Hence *base*ball.

He watches a first-base hit.

Hmm. Like circular cricket.

AUDREY

I guess.

GILES

Is there something wrong, Audrey?

Pause.

AUDREY

We're going to see my folks tomorrow. Up in Vermont.

Ronnie comes to bat; they both lean forward, for a better look.

GILES

Vermont?

AUDREY

For a week.

GILES

A week.

AUDREY

Before Ron has to go back . . .

Ronnie misses his first pitch.

That's a strike, Giles.

GILES

To, er, Los Angeles?

AUDREY

Right.

GILES

Ronnie never mentioned this.

AUDREY

He doesn't know yet.

GILES

You understand, we have a lot of work to do on the script?

AUDREY

That's too bad. I guess he'll get by . . .

Ronnie misses his second ball.

That's a strike, too, Giles.

GILES

Audrey, surely it's as clear to you as it is to me that he deserves much more than 'getting by'?

Audrey watches Ronnie limber up.

AUDREY

He'll do it this time. He never gets struck out. Watch this, Giles. It's gonna be a good one; the bases are loaded.

GILES

You realise this is a crucial moment in his life?

AUDREY

God, you're good . . .

Her words hang in the air. Ronnie lunges desperately and sends the ball curving into a glorious arc. They are suddenly united in their excitement. Ronnie starts to run with absolute determination.

AUDREY
(*triumphantly*)

That's a home run, Giles!

She turns slowly to look at Giles, but he cannot tear himself away from Ronnie flying round the bases, the epitome of youthful exuberance. It is an exquisite performance.

INT. MOTEL ROOM – DAY

Giles is packing hurriedly. As he tosses his sports jacket into the suitcase, something slides out of a pocket: the sunglasses Ronnie lent him on the day in the Hamptons.

He opens them delicately, as if touching the head they once encircled.

He cannot stop himself picking up the phone. He dials a number he knows by heart, and waits a long time for it to be answered.

> GILES
> (*softly*)

Ronnie?

INT. CHEZ D'IRV – DUSK

Irv listens to a baseball game on the radio. Giles, very agitated, smokes while watching the door.

> IRV

You like baseball, Giles?

> GILES

I'm afraid it's defeated me . . .

Irv turns the radio off.

Cricket is more my . . . As a boy, I knew every detail.

> IRV

Like what?

> GILES

Oh, the Ashes; that kind of thing.

> IRV

Is that a fact?

> GILES

Oh, yes. Let's see now . . . England 1953: Hutton (captain),

Edrich, May, Compton, Graveney, Bailey, Evans, Laker, Lock, Bedser and of course Freddie Trueman.

As Giles recites the names, Ronnie enters in sunglasses.

IRV

Incredible.

LOU

He could just be making them up.

IRV

Hey, the Professor's always right.

RONNIE
(*sitting*)

You showing off again?

GILES
(*smiling*)

Not at all. It's good of you to come, Ronnie. Let me get you something. I'm afraid Irving has yet to discover de-caff, but –

IRV
(*approaching their booth*)

Can I get your friend something?

GILES

Irving, this is Ronnie Bostock, a young actor I've been working with. Ronnie, Irving Buckmuller.

IRV
(*shaking Ronnie's hand*)

Any friend of Giles' is welcome here. What'll it be?

RONNIE

Diet coke.

IRV

Coming right up.

GILES

Surely you don't have to watch your weight?

RONNIE

Nope. Tastes better . . . You really are Mr Popular, aren't you?

GILES

People here have been very kind.

RONNIE

Aud said even the woman selling our house had met you!

GILES
(*thrown*)

Oh, did she?

He looks at Ronnie's eyes, but all he sees is his own reflection in his sunglasses.

Ronnie, could you possibly take off your sunglasses?

RONNIE

Sure.

GILES

That's better.

RONNIE
(*sharply*)

Giles! You've just got to stop!

Customers look round from the counter.

GILES
(*alarmed*)

I'm sorry?

Ronnie pushes away the brimming ashtray.

RONNIE

You gotta cut down, at least.

GILES

Oh . . . I appreciate your concern.

The diet coke arrives.

So. This is your last day in Long Island . . . Or does one say *on* Long Island?

RONNIE

Whatever . . . Yeah, Aud's got real kinda antsy, so . . .

GILES

I'll also be leaving Long Island soon.

RONNIE

Yeah? Maybe we could touch base in Europe some time?

GILES

I'd like that, Ronnie. I'd like that very much.

Pause.

You must of course honour your obligations to Audrey, but it strikes me that you're very young to be making such a commitment, especially with your career at this crucial stage.

RONNIE

Yeah, well. A guy should know when he's onto a good thing. Wasn't it like that for you?

GILES

Well, er, I suppose so, yes.

As Ronnie takes a swig, Giles catches sight of his mole. His resigned mood vanishes.

RONNIE

It's a birthmark. They cover it up for shooting, but I kinda like it.

GILES

You know, I always thought it was on the right.

RONNIE

How d'you mean?

Pause.

GILES
(*dropping his voice*)
Ronnie, I have a confession to make. I've been waiting for you
for quite some time.

RONNIE
(*looking at his watch*)
Hey, I'm sorry. I had to drop Aud off, and –

GILES

For several years, in fact.

RONNIE

How d'you mean?

Pause.

GILES
(*with gravitas*)
There is nothing more solitary than an artist's life, Ronnie. No
doubt you'll discover that for yourself – painfully, perhaps.
One yearns for solace without quite knowing where to look
for it. But I found it in you – much more than you will ever
know.

RONNIE

Yeah? Hey, that's great.

GILES

Ronnie, I have another confession to make. I've brought you
here not to say goodbye, but to make you an offer.

RONNIE

An offer?

GILES

I'm prepared to devote myself to your career.

RONNIE
(*smiling*)
I really appreciate all this, Giles. You gotta come out west some time and –

GILES
(*impassioned*)
Ronnie, you must forget Los Angeles – put it behind you. Your future lies in Europe.

RONNIE
Hey, this has been a great ego trip, Giles, but I gotta take one step at a time. Aud wants to work in Europe again, and it would sure be cool to spend time there, but –

GILES
Cool!? I'm talking about a turning-point in your life!

RONNIE
I got no contacts there. People know me here; I'm doing OK.

GILES
As what, Ronnie? As what?

RONNIE
(*a little hurt*)
Let's keep in touch, huh? Are you close to finishing that script?

Pause.

GILES
Listen to me, Ronnie. In Europe, it's very often the case that a young man benefits from the wisdom and experience of an elder. Why, there's practically a tradition of such friendships. Our art's dominated by such creative endeavours: Cocteau and Radiquet; Verlaine and Rimbaud –

RONNIE
(*incredulous*)

Rambo?!

GILES
(*patiently*)

Arthur Rimbaud. The French poet. He was Paul Verlaine's
lover.

*Ronnie's eyes die a little. He leans back, empties the can and looks
at his watch.*

RONNIE
(*flustered*)

Shoot! I gotta go. Aud'll be wondering where I am. I don't
want another fight.

GILES
(*shriller*)

Listen – I do understand your misgivings and I respect the fact
that your immediate plans are founded on these . . .
temporary attachments.

RONNIE

What?

GILES

Ronnie, your relationship with Audrey is hardly likely to last
for ever.

RONNIE
(*quietly*)

Why not?

GILES

I . . . I'm afraid it's obvious to me.

RONNIE
(*louder*)

What are you trying to say?

GILES
(*looking round*)
Ronnie, please . . .

RONNIE
Giles, I'd like to think you meant what you said about my
work, but you've got things all wrong. Me and Aud, we're a
team.

GILES
(*seizing his hand*)
Ronnie. Ronnie. Listen to me. You don't understand . . .

RONNIE
I think I do.
(*looking round, embarrassed*)
I'm outta here.

GILES
How can you act like this, when you know – you *must* know
– how completely., how desperately . . . I love you.

*Ronnie looks up in astonishment. He gazes at Giles almost
tenderly, with a strange kind of respect. Bereft of words, Giles
savours the moment.*

*But it is suddenly broken. Ronnie's expression hardens into
blankness. He pulls his hand gently from Giles' grasp and puts his
sunglasses back on. Giles stares at his reflection in them as Ronnie
rises, touches him briefly on the shoulder and leaves.*

Dear God. What have I done?

*He buries his face in his hands. Irv discreetly turns the baseball
game back on; a gesture of sympathy.*

EXT. A JETTY – DUSK

Giles looks down at the waves, a desolate figure in the landscape.

INT./EXT. MOTEL – NIGHT

Giles' fountain-pen swirls across the paper.

He writes with real passion, his hand as elegant as ever, but hurried. His expression ranges from tenderness to frenzied pain, but the process is an immense release to him.

The pages mount up through the night.

EXT. MOTEL FORECOURT – DAY

At dawn, an 'Oyster Bay' taxi pulls up.

EXT. THE BEACH – DAY

Identical to the opening scene: Ronnie leads Strider back to the Porsche.

EXT. THE UPLANDS – DAY

As before: the Mailman leaves his jeep to make deliveries; an elderly jogger passes by; a woman walks her dog; a boy hurls papers into front gardens from his bike; kids hurry to a school-bus.

EXT. RONNIE'S HOUSE – DAY

The taxi stops beside Ronnie's mailbox. Audrey suddenly steps out of the garage and looks at them suspiciously.

GILES
(*alarmed*)

Drive on!

EXT. THE UPLANDS – DAY

The taxi stops in front of the Mailman's jeep.

GILES

Good morning. I wonder if you could do me a great favour and add this to your deliveries?

MAILMAN

I'm not sure I can do that, sir.

He looks at the address.

It's just around the corner.

GILES

It has to be, er, something of a surprise. Maybe I could . . .

He takes money from his pocket.

MAILMAN

I can't do that, sir. It's a federal offense.

GILES

But surely . . .

MAILMAN

I'm sorry, sir.

EXT. RONNIE'S HOUSE – DAY

As Ronnie turns into the drive, a delivery is made to his mailbox.

EXT./INT. A STATIONARY STORE – DAY

The taxi waits outside as Giles tears open the envelope and slaps a huge pile of paper on the counter.

GILES
(*agitated*)
I would like this sent as a 'fax' . . .

He fumbles for Ronnie's business card.

. . . to this number.

FAX ASSISTANT
(*thumbing through the pile*)
All of it?

> GILES

Every word.

> FAX ASSISTANT

It's gonna take a while.

> GILES

I'm prepared to leave it with you.

INT. RONNIE'S LIVING ROOM – DAY

The fax machine rings and purrs into action. Ronnie walks over aimlessly and starts to read:

> GILES
> (*voice-over*)

My dear Ronnie. It is so difficult to know where I should begin; especially when, unlike you, I already know the ending. But let us say that this story began with the end of another, far, far from the surf of Long Island . . .

He stops and glances out of the window at Audrey hosing plants, then reads on.

INT. THE TAXI – DAY

The taxi joins a highway. The Cab Driver studies Giles in the mirror. He is smiling with creative satisfaction, his composure regained.

He finds his passport and tickets in a pocket. With them is an unfamiliar object – a cigarette filter. Its packaging bears the legend 'Cut Down in Style!' Ronnie has written in a corner: 'For Giles – you gotta stop!'

Giles is touched by the gesture. He unwraps the filter delicately and twirls it in his fingers as if it were his fountain-pen.

> CAB DRIVER 3

You can't smoke in here, sir.

INT. RONNIE'S LIVING ROOM – DAY

Pages continue to pour from the machine. We follow their trail to Ronnie, sitting reading on the floor. He is utterly enthralled.

We see a fast, seamless montage of what he reads: Giles smoking in the London taxi; Ronnie's name in the credit roll; a newsagents; a pint of UHT milk; the TV delivery; the scrapbook being named 'Bostockiana'.

Audrey glances round the door. He looks up (but not at her) with a dazed smile.

> AUDREY
>
> What's all that?

Pause.

> RONNIE
> (*from far away*)
>
> Rewrites.

> AUDREY
> (*disappearing*)
>
> Those guys are never gonna get it right.

INT. THE TAXI – DAY

The taxi gathers speed on a freeway. Giles taps the filter rhythmically on his knee, staring ahead. His resolute expression falters. His eyes gradually fill with tears.

INT. RONNIE'S LIVING ROOM – DAY

Ronnie now sits reading on the couch. The dog lopes in for attention but is ignored.

We see a montage of what he reads: Giles arriving at Chesterton Station; spotting the Porsche; then Strider; being shown around Ronnie's house; crashing into Audrey's shopping cart . . .

Ronnie looks up and laughs out loud.

INT. THE TAXI – DAY

Giles smiles, as if in response to Ronnie's laughter. He catches the Cab Driver's eye in the mirror.

> GILES
> (*slowly*)
> Tell me . . . When one sends a 'fax' . . . Is there any way it can be, er, reversed?

> CAB DRIVER 3
> How d'you mean, sir?

> GILES
> Well, can it be 'got back'?

> CAB DRIVER 3
> I don't know about that.

> GILES
> I would imagine not.

Pause.

Cab Driver 3 glances at him tolerantly.

> CAB DRIVER 3
> You wanna turn back?

> GILES
> I think it's rather too late for that.

He chuckles to himself.

> CAB DRIVER 3
> You sure?

> GILES
> Quite sure, thank you.

INT. RONNIE'S LIVING ROOM – DAY

The fax machine is now silent. Giles' letter creates a tangled trail across the floor, with Strider asleep over part of it. Ronnie reaches the last page:

GILES
(*voice-over*)

Well, Ronnie, there it is, the end of our story. And also the beginning of a new story for me – but perhaps you've worked that out for yourself. But what of you, my darling? For no one on earth knows you better than I do, and if you've read thus far, I know you'll never bring yourself to destroy this letter. Nor will you ever show it to anyone else; to Audrey in particular . . .

Ronnie's expression changes, demonstrating the vulnerability so familiar from his films.

And it will gradually dawn on you that your life might have taken a very different course, had you simply been able to open your heart to another. And you'll often return to this letter. You'll read it again and again in the years to come, until you no longer have to read what you'll know by heart. And you'll cherish it as a source of pride in the face of an uncaring world . . .

Pause.

Ronnie lifts his head to look far into the distance. Lying on the couch, he drops one arm to the ground, the end of the fax curling onto the floor.

The image bears an uncanny resemblance to Wallis' painting of Chatterton and Ronnie's fate in the pizza parlor of Hotpants College.

He suddenly leaps up and violently scrunches the fax pages into a ball.

He stops just as suddenly, and gently starts to smooth the pages out. His hands stop on the only page in typescript: the scene that Giles typed in the motel for his new film.

EXT./INT. THE TAXI – DAY

The taxi crosses a bridge. Sunlight flickers across its girders and creates a repetitive play of light and shade on Giles' face.

With a little aplomb, he reaches into his pocket and puts on the youthful sunglasses that Ronnie lent him during their Hamptons day.

They now seem to reveal rather than conceal; they become an affirmation of his adventure, a fusion of his and Ronnie's cultures.

He leans back as if he has travelled a great distance indeed. A wry smile crosses his lips.

EXT./INT. A CINEMA – DAY

A cinema's billing shows: 'SPECIAL PREVIEW: Hotpants College III'.

Inside, the projector beam flickers with the colours of a thousand fantasies.

Over the heads of the audience, we see a scene from the film:

On screen:

EXT. GRAVEYARD – DAY

Ronnie (as Mikey) stands at his mother's grave, surrounded by the familiar Hotpants cast.

RONNIE
I'd like to say a few words, if that's OK with everyone . . .

He pulls out a crumpled piece of paper.

'Now finale to the shore,

12: **Hotpants 3 (b)**

Now land and life finale and farewell.
The untold want by life and land never granted,
Now voyager sail thou forth to seek and find.'

*Although this is virtually identical to the scene imagined by Giles,
Ronnie's performance is now genuinely moving.*

*As he replaces his baseball cap, the cast members nod to each
other. One of them pats Ronnie on the back. Another murmurs
'Way to go, Mikey'.*

*Ronnie looks up over the camera, his face imbued with a certain
serenity.*

ROLL CREDITS.

POST-SCRIPT
A conversation between Gilbert Adair, Richard Kwietniowski and Mark Sinker.

MS: Gilbert, what did you learn about your book that you didn't know before you saw the film?
GA: The most important discovery for me was that it was *filmable*. I initially didn't think it was at all. I was quite happy to take the option money, happy to be invited to lunch, happy to spend the day with Richard talking about the project, but I really didn't believe the novel had much cinematic potential. It just didn't strike me as visual enough. Everything, after all, takes place inside the protagonist's head, so that the reader knows only what the narrator elects to let him know.

To take a specific example: Giles, this middle-aged man who never goes to the cinema, goes one day, almost by chance. He finds himself watching a film that he never intended to see and is smitten with a young male actor whom he considers to be spectacularly beautiful. In the book, though, the reader has to take Ronnie's beauty entirely on faith. There's absolutely no guarantee that the boy is objectively beautiful. In Richard's film, on the other hand, his appearance becomes as much of an objective given as Giles' own.

When Richard and I talked about casting, I asked whether I might be consulted on the choice of performer for the role, because there was something of Giles in me and something of me in Giles. There was no contractual obligation on his part. He'd bought the rights and he could cast who he pleased. But it was the one element in the novel in which there was, if you like, a profound investment of self. However, as far as Ronnie is concerned, I said it's *your* camera that's got to love him. Although I was naturally interested to know who it would eventually be, I felt the casting of Ronnine had to be entirely Richard's decision; his vision, his fantasy.

To come back to your question, what I learned was that

extremely subjective literary material could be appropriated by a film director and made subjective – *subjective to him* – all over again. I hadn't believed that could be done.

MS: *Richard, what grabbed you about the book?*
RK: Reviews I read talked enthusiastically about it as a story about the cinema transforming someone's life, and about its playfulness, which I associate with Gilbert's writing. So I bought it – in hardback, unusually – along with two or three paperbacks, my monthly quota to help me sleep, and – even more unusually – read it in one go. I think even during that first reading I was imagining what it could be like as a film, partly because it connected in so many ways with me.

The whole idea of two cultures coming together, for instance, is very much my personal history; being English, but growing up with a Polish immigrant father and having a displaced relationship with a lot of British culture. I also grew up being very fascinated by aspects of American popular culture, which plays a large part in the book.

I especially like stories about obsession, the irrational, about taking desire in a direction where there are no rules. Some of my favourite films are about this. Most important was the playfulness, which very much connected with the type of film I want to make. It was the key element I thought I could possibly extend.

MS: *Did it tell you things about film you hadn't thought of before?*
RK: Yes, in the sense that the project involved quite a lot of guesswork. I think there's not much point in doing something you're 100% confident about. You're asking not just backers but also cast and crew to invest in something that represents a number of risks. For instance, would our casting combination work? Should it be able to work? One of the reasons why I wanted to do it was to see if you *could* make a film on both sides of the Atlantic, about the two cultures meeting, and with many reflexive elements such as films within the film.

The process of adapting the book entailed a lot of thinking about how cinema can genuinely expand on elements – tonal elements, within a novel – and how it can render them visually; how it *has* to. For instance, to show time has passed and that Giles' obsession with Ronnie, this B-movie actor, has become a very important part of his life, I wrote a scene where he imagines he's on a TV quiz show, answering specialised questions on 'The Life and Work of Ronnie Bostock'. Suddenly the script takes on an additional element, *visualising* the main character's fantasy life.

MS: *Gilbert, in your essay on having this novel turned into a film, you too said something about latent relationships being brought out . . .*

GA: The first time Richard presented me with a script, he said, 'What I've tried to do is open the narrative out.' I accepted he'd had to do this because, as I said, my belief had been that it was unfilmable. He also said, 'I know you're going to worry about certain aspects of the script, but what I've basically done is take elements from the novel and expand them. I haven't sought to invent new characters, new settings, new sequences.' And I thought to myself, 'Yeah, yeah, yeah, I've heard that before'.

That first draft had a number of things wrong with it, as I'm sure Richard will agree. But (a) I was immediately convinced that, yes, he was going to make this film; and (b) I was amazed to discover he'd done exactly what he'd claimed to have done. Take the deaf woman who lives next door to Giles. In the novel she's less a character than merely an allusion. She's important because she gives Giles the idea for a novel with a deaf-mute protagonist, which is, on a latent or symbolic level, what Giles is in my own novel – I didn't want to make heavy weather of that in the book and I don't want to make heavy weather of it now, but she is absolutely not alive on the page. Richard turned this 'allusion' into a character who has a real presence on the screen.

The most radical example of what I'm talking about is the fact that no more than thirty pages of my novel are actually set on Long Island, whereas it's the setting of half the film. The characters of Audrey and Irv, the motel in which Giles stays, Giles' relationship with Ronnie are – in a sense – all in the book, but

Richard has permitted them to expand on the screen, like a Japanese paper flower in water.

RK: One thing I very much wanted to expand on was this idea of a fan developing a false intimacy with an idol, through the power of images – moving and still – that the fan can track down and possess. I knew this could be very powerfully conveyed in the film, by staging scenes from the movies Giles watches Ronnie in, by seeing images of him in magazines, and so on. I wanted to fetishize Ronnie's presence as a representation, to convey Giles' state of mind.

For instance, the second time Giles goes to the cinema to see *Hotpants College II*, the scene where Ronnie's humiliated in the pizza parlor appears to be shot differently from the first time we saw it. Now there's a camera move from Ronnie's feet to his face. There's a certain confusion about whether such a shot is actually in *Hotpants College II*, or whether we're seeing this through Giles' eyes. In a sense it's obviously the latter, but it's protected by the existence of the former, the fact that we are apparently watching an extract, on screen, of this terrible teen sex comedy.

It seemed very important to suggest it is possible to look at a film very subjectively, to see something there that no one else has seen. It's a bit like freeze-framing a video and creating a temporary image that seems to have nothing to do with the actual film, which Giles also does once he has gone through the troublesome process of learning how to operate a VCR. It was tricky filming the films within the film, these cheesy B-movies Ronnie is in. I didn't want to just parody them. I wanted them to feel authentic, but also to suggest someone could find something special in them, something personal, almost by accident.

GA: If I could offer a little anecdote here. One of the earliest scenes to be shot was at the Coronet cinema in Notting Hill, which is where Giles sees *Hotpants College II*. Since it's just around the corner from where I live, Richard rang me up and said, 'Why don't you come along and have a look?' So I did, and it was a very strange and rather wonderful experience for me to see this cinema, which I know well, and also to see on its marquee the title

Hotpants College II, a film I'd completely invented. They'd taken down the poster for whatever had been showing there and replaced it with a poster for this imaginary film.

I went to see the shooting, and then it broke up for lunch and I had to do some shopping. When I returned, the equipment was there, the usual vans were there, but everyone was still at lunch. I happened to see this fellow stroll up to the Coronet and start to examine the poster for *Hotpants College II*. He stood there for the longest time, and I thought, no, this is too humiliating. I simply can't let him go in and ask to buy a ticket. So I finally approached him and said, 'I'm afraid you've misunderstood . . . a film is being shot here . . . this is just, you know . . .' He was so embarrassed he went totally red in the face, since he'd been looking at the poster for quite a while and possibly thinking. 'What's this? Maybe I *do* want to see *Hotpants College II*.' It just confirms what you were saying about the ambiguities of illusion. If the poster had been left there long enough, probably the cinema would have started to fill up.

RK: There were a number of interesting overlaps between reality and illusion throughout the shoot, especially concerning the casting of heart-throb Jason Priestley as heart-throb Ronnie Bostock. In one scene, two teenage fans stop Ronnie and ecstatically ask for his autograph, and it occurred to me, why do we need to stage this? It happens every day. Fans stop *Jason* and ecstatically ask for his autograph.

That's one reason why I wanted to cast him, because I thought he would know everything about the obligations of an idol to a fan, about this strange false intimacy that exists. As an actor he would be able not only to be playful with his own image, but also to allow his character to grow in a certain way.

GA: It's interesting watching how Jason, playing this character which in some way relates to his own career, puts inverted commas around himself. Frankly, I would never have expected him to do it as skilfully and movingly as he does. He gets right inside the character but also manages to distance himself from it. The sign of a real actor!

MS: *In a different novel, in which a 14-year-old girl has a crush on Ronnie, she could have no resources to enact any of this. However, someone with some sort of cultural power – albeit in a different world – someone who can actually manoeuvre this encounter, is someone who can turn it into a real love story, rather than a purely imaginary one. This brings home – very forcefully in the book because it's the last line, but also in the film – the destructive power of fandom. Ronnie's gentleness with this particular fan is surely part of this: you have to be a little indulgent towards fans, because they created you and they can also tear you limb from limb, like Orpheus and the Maenads.*

GA: I've always been fascinated by the expression 'to fall in love', fascinated by the notion that love is something you *fall* into. With actors like Jason Priestley, Leonardo DiCaprio and Keanu Reeves, we expect that the only types liable to fall in love with them are immature little girls (or not so immature and, indeed, not so little boys). We tend to believe that no one of a certain age or intelligence or experience could possibly be interested in them. I don't accept that at all. We don't always choose appropriate objects of desire for ourselves. As far as I'm concerned, love is something you control only up to a point – then it starts to control you.

That's why the novel is, for me, exclusively Giles' story. It's the story of a man who not only falls in love but falls *into* love. Whereas Richard's film is ultimately about the emotional interaction of *two* people, Giles and Ronnie. Ronnie's response to Giles becomes just as intriguing to the spectator as Giles' to Ronnie. The inside of Ronnie's head simply does not exist in the book, and that's a fundamental difference between novel and film.

RK: I wanted the film to be as interested in the object of adoration. It's quite complex being a star, a heart-throb. Everywhere Ronnie goes – and Jason Priestley, as well – people think they know him, claim to love him, offer him love, whether it's teenage girls or middle-aged English authors. And this love is something he – or any heart-throb – is unable to return. All they can do is absorb or deflect it. It seemed interesting to suggest there could be a mutual and fairly equal exchange between these two people from different continents, different cultures, different generations, because they're both incomplete. I ultimately wanted to suggest that both characters grow, by becoming a little more like each other.

MS: *Yes. The actor's world is shaken by* this *fan, this fan he can admire. He's flattered in a way that he can no longer be, except in the abstract, by all the girls. Jason's had eight years of that as Brandon in Beverly Hills 90210, and Ronnie's had however many years of it, so his response, even at the moment of rejection, still has to be very complicated. He doesn't want it just to be flattery. He doesn't want all the nice things Giles said to be just a way of this old guy getting into bed with him. Which brings to a head this very complicated relationship that all of us have with the screen, with different people on the screen. Complicated passions for idols which can often have a very intellectual base are often exactly the opposite.*

GA: Friends of mine who've seen and liked the film have said to me, 'The ending is very different. Aren't you troubled by that?' I suppose I was troubled, obscurely, at first. Then I thought to myself – my train of thought may seem a trifle circuitous here, but we'll get to the point eventually – if you wear dark grey trousers, say, and a jacket which is also grey, *but not exactly the same grey*, it looks naff and awkward, doesn't it? Almost as though you were hoping to pass it off as a suit. Far better to wear a jacket in a different colour altogether. I rather think film adaptations are like that. If the film and novel were too similar, it would be like trying to match a pair of grey trousers with a jacket of a dissimilar shade of grey. It pleases me that, using the same basic pool or kitty of narrative elements, Richard and I have contrived to produce very different kinds of fiction. My novel and his film are twins, if you like, but not identical twins.

MS: *What was it like having Giles – a character you'd invented – played by John Hurt?*
GA: For me, as I said before, Giles is something of an *alter ego*. That name, to begin with! When I learned that John Hurt had

agreed to play him, I was absolutely enchanted. Then when I saw the film, I felt that, if I possessed even a fraction of his elegance and style and behavioural charm, I could accept just about everything that life had to throw at me. In a way, it mirrors what I've just been saying about the differences between the novel and film. My Giles and John's Giles are twins, but, just as in the kind of old Bette Davis melodrama that both Richard and I adore, John's Giles is the *nice* twin.

RK: That's one reason why the film had to end differently, with affirmation, rather than revenge. The book's ending is astonishing because it's completely speculative. Giles writes a letter to Ronnie in which he tells him this letter will destroy him. Does Giles really believe so much in the power of his pen? Does he really want to destroy him? Will Ronnie even read the letter? It's devilishly effective as a literary ending, but wouldn't work at all for a film.

I think there's an inexorable logic about the way most films tell stories. I knew an audience would always be aware of the fact that these two characters would not ultimately walk into the sunset together, but I wanted to end the story in a way that definitely affirmed Giles' *coming out*, his emergence into a life enriched by emotion and even love. Yet I wanted to do so in a way that was a little surprising.

I toyed with elements that were already in the book, such as enlarging the role of Ronnie's girlfriend Audrey, and the way Fiona Loewi plays that part definitely makes it crucial in the final act. I eventually stumbled on the idea of doing something directly about Ronnie and Giles stepping into each other's cultures. There's a scene we see which Giles has written for Ronnie, where he recites Walt Whitman – very well and with great significance – and then there's its mirror-image: a scene where Giles reads lines from the new *Hotpants* script with Ronnie and has to negotiate American teen-speak – 'Hey, dude, how's it hanging?' – and so on. Of course there's the additional pleasure of hearing someone of John Hurt's stature having to say such lines, but the character he plays has developed a certain fascination for Ronnie's culture, for its energy and directness and also, of course, for its 'Ronnieness'. So there's a beneficial exchange between the two characters, even at the level of learning the language of each other's culture.

GA: There was one point on which we were in total agreement from the beginning, which was that there should be no crass so-called satire of American vulgarity. The truth is that, in my novel, and to a greater extent in the film, Giles *likes* America. And America likes Giles. There may be a collision of cultures and personalities, but there's also the sense that America offers Giles the freedom to explore his own feelings more honestly than he'd ever been able to in England. The American experience is mostly fruitful and positive, and I think that's something that gives the film its very original charm. I was amused to see that certain American reviewers made a point of contrasting the rather waspish and sarcastic individuals Giles encounters in London with the Long Islanders he meets, who are all very kind and sweet to him.

RK: But that's the way I've always found America.

GA: Yet so many British writers and film-makers continue to peddle the same old pseudo-Jamesian opposition of the two cultures.

RK: We've talked before about the ending of Gus Van Sant's *My Own Private Idaho*, when River Phoenix's character – the narcoleptic – collapses in the road. A truck stops and they steal his boots, his wallet, his jacket, and drive off. Then a second truck stops and the driver takes him in his arms and drives him away. So many other film-makers wouldn't have had that second truck and we'd have been left yet again with the message that the US is such a heartless place.

GA: The film is absolutely free of condescension. Even with the film-within-the-film parodies, with the movies Giles watches, one senses an affection. They're truly terrible, of course, but everyone in them gives of their best and, just occasionally, something gets through to you. Everything in Giles resists such tripe, yet it pierces his armour. Certain American reviewers found it a very unusual British film because there's an evident sympathy with – almost a love of – the textures of American popular culture.

153

RK: When I looked at films like the ones Ronnie appears in – *Porky's*, *The Last American Virgin*, *Lemon Popsicle* – I found some surprising elements. You don't know whether someone consciously put them there, or whether they snookered themselves a bit in telling the story. For instance, there are some contradictory things. There's always more male than female nudity, yet I assume these films are made for teenage guys. Some do try the occasional profundity. Hard-nosed realities come into play in the third act, such as abortion. They change tone in strange ways.

I certainly wanted to suggest there are things in popular culture that you can personalize and view subjectively. I remember when a friend was an extra in *One From the Heart*. I saw a completely different film to the rest of the audience because every time there was a crowd scene – and there are many – I was scanning the corners of the frame, examining everything out of focus, to catch a glimpse of her. I had to go and see the film again in order to see the actual film.

For Giles, *Hotpants* is always about Ronnie, even when he is out of focus, as it were, but it also introduces him to this completely impenetrable culture that he comes to be very energised by. I think the film is ultimately saying something very straightforward – that difference is good. To be alive is to respond to difference, to allow yourself to be stimulated by difference: different cultures, languages, continents, ways of life, generations, and, yes, different desires, sexualities, sensibilities.

Giles is effectively dead in London because he doesn't allow himself to come into contact with anything he doesn't understand. This is why he doesn't have a television. When he goes to Long Island, everything changes, as if he stops *watching*, and climbs up onto the screen and becomes an active participant. It's significant, of course, that Giles' life is transformed by something that happens in a cinema, and that sexuality is the key that opens the door to new continents, including desire. The story begins with the repression of homosexuality, but becomes something a lot more universal, about permitting love to enrich and transform your life, perhaps. I know that was very important to John Hurt. It was a major reason why he took the part and also why he was able to imbue the role with so much that seems to touch people very deeply – the humour as well as the pathos.

CREDITS

Corey	VINCENT CORAZZA
Brad	GEOFFREY HEROD
Tommy	RYAN ROGERSON
Big Guy	BRUCE FILLMORE
Corey's Mother	NANCY MARSHALL
The Stomper	ELIZABETH MURPHY
Molly	JENNIE RAYMOND
Rusty	CHARLES JANNASCH
Pete	SHAUN D. RICHARDSON
Jake	GABRIEL HOGAN
Father Bryson	JEREMY AKERMAN
Sitcom Mother	CHRISTINE JEFFERS
Sitcom Father	MORRISSEY DUNN
Strider	SWAYZEE
Mrs Reed's Dog	OUZO

CREW

Director/screenplay writer	RICHARD KWIETNIOWSKI
Producers	STEVE CLARK-HALL
	CHRISTOPHER ZIMMER
Based on the novel by	GILBERT ADAIR
Director of Photography	OLIVER CURTIS
Editor	SUSAN SHIPTON
Music	THE INSECTS
	RICHARD GRASSBY-LEWIS
Trumpet soloist	JON HASSELL
Designer	DAVID MCHENRY
Costume Designer	ANDREA GALER
	MARTHA CURRY
Make-up Designer	TORY WRIGHT
Casting	KATE DAY
	JON COMERFORD
Associate Producer	BRIAN DONOVAN
1st Assistant Director	MAX KEENE
Script Supervisor	MAGGIE THOMAS
Additional Casting	JOHN DUNSWORTH (Halifax)
	CHRISTINE SHEAKS (Los Angeles)

LONDON CREW

<pre>
   Production Manager   MAIRI BETT
         Art Director   FLEUR WHITLOCK
         Sound Mixer   NEIL KINGSBURY
     Location Manager   MARTELL
               Gaffer   TERRY HUNT
         Focus Puller   MARK SILK
       Clapper Loader   STEVEN CASSIDY
       Video Playback   ROB DICKINSON
       Camera Trainee   ZENA HOLLOWAY
   FT2/Camera Trainee   JAKE HULL
   Stills Photographer SOPHIE BAKER
                 Grip   DENNIS DILLON
      Standby Rigging   ALFIE BLORE
        Boom Operator   JAYA BISHOP
    FT2/Sound Trainee   REBECCA BUCKLEY
Production Co-ordinator EMMA JAMES
</pre>

2nd Assistant Director	FINN MCGRATH
3rd Assistant Director	JEZ MURRELL
Location Assistant	COLIN PLENTY
Production Runner	BARTHOLOMEW BAKER
Floor Runner	JON HOWE
Production Accountant	JANE KEARNEY-COLLINS
Accounts Assistant	CHARLOTTE FARRAR
Storyboard Artist	PAUL RUXTON
Art Department Co-ordinator	JAMES L. WOLSTENHOLME
Property Buyer	BARRY GREAVES
Property Master	JOHN ALLENBY
Dressing Props	ROY O'CONNOR
Standby Props	ROBERT HILL
	STEVE MCDONALD
Best Boy Electrician	DARREN HARVEY
Electricians	LEN O'BRIEN
	DICK CONWAY
	PAUL DALEY
Wardrobe	DIANE MURPHY
	TIM GUTHRIE
Make-up Assistant	C. J. WILLS
Stand-ins	JACK ROSS
	CLAIR CHRYSLER
Unit Nurse	DEBBIE HARKINS
Construction Manager	DAVE BALL
Standby Carpenter	RICKY BURNETT
Standby Painter	JASON REILLY
Mr Hurt's Driver	TONY JAYES
Unit Driver	JERRY FLOYD
Props Runaround Driver	KENNY LUPTON
Props Standby Driver	LES QUICK
Make-up Bus Driver	DAVID ELLIS
Wardrobe Bus Driver	CHARLIE SIMPSON
Camera Car Driver	ROBERT FOWLE

NOVA SCOTIA CREW

Production Manager	GILLES BELANGER
Art Director	EMMANUEL JANNASCH
Sound Mixer	JIM RILLIE
Boom Operator	ALEX SALTER
Location Manager	GARY SWIM
Gaffer	MARIO PAULIN
1st Assistant Camera	FORBES MACDONALD
2nd Assistant Camera	JOHN COCHRANE
Camera Trainee	KYLE CAMERON
Video Assistant Operator	CHUCK CALKER
EPK Camera	FRED MACDONALD
Stills Photographer	CHRIS REARDON
Grips	CHUCK CLARK
	MAYNARD HARRIS
	CAROLYN ADAMS
	STEVE ARNOLD

	PAUL MITCHELTREE
	TODD MURCHIE
Key Grip	JEFF ADAMS
Best Boy Grip	KEITH ADAMS
Standby Rigging	JOSEPH RICK GILLIS
	STEPHAN GLENN GILLIS
Boom Operator	ALEX SALTER
Production Co-ordinator	KARLA MORASH
Assistant Co-ordinator	DEREK FILIATRAULT
2nd Assistant Director	SHANDI MITCHELL-MACLEOD
3rd Assistant Director	MARY REYNOLDS
Location Assistant	DAVID HYSLOP
Production Runner	ANDREA DORFMAN
Floor Runner	BARBARA BADESSI
Production Accountant	ELIZABETH KAVANAGH
Accounts Assistant	ANDREA KOKIC
Assistant Art Director	JENNIFER STEWART
Property Master	TERESITA DOUCET-REILLY
Assistant Props	PAUL GORMAN
	CLAUDE ROUSSEL
Set Decorator	PATRICIA LARMAN
Set Buyer	MARY STECKLE
Set Dresser	LORNE ARMSTRONG
	ROB GRANI
Assistant Set Decorators	GREG ALLEN
	SCOTT SIMPSON
	BILL HARDWICK
	JASON SHURKO
Best Boy Electrician	JAKE CLARKE
Genny Operator	JAN MEYEROWITZ
Electricians	JAMES THIBODEAU
	RUTH LEGGETT
	WARD SWAN
	ERIC EMERY
Wardrobe	PATRICIA COWMEADOW
	CARA PORTER
Make-up Stylist	CATHY O'CONNELL
Hair Stylist	NORMA RICHARD
Make-up Assistant	KIM ROSS

Utility Runners	JARI-MATTI HELPPI
	LAURI HUYGHUE
Construction Manager	RICHARD FRASER
Carpenters	MICHAEL HIGGINS
	CHRISTIAN SULLIVAN
	CHRIS HILL
	GLEN MCELMON
	DARREN NAUSS
Scenic	BRENARD FAYE
	JAMES TUMBLIN
	TONY OWEN
	KENDRICK BECK
	MARILYN MCAVOY
	DAVID MARSH
	DANIEL DELAQUIS
Assistant Scenic/Painters	JAMES D'AMBROGI
	GEORGE GORE
	ADAM HALLETT
Stunt Co-ordinator	BRANKO RACKI
Stunt Double	JOHN STONEHAM JR
Animal Wrangler	KIM MURRAY
Transport Co-ordinator	MICHAEL SULLIVAN
Transport Captain	MANNY TAYLOR
Vehicle Wrangler	DARLENE SHIELS
Mr Hurt's Driver	JACK NIVEN
Mr Priestley's Driver	HAL SHAVER
Unit Drivers	JOHN VAN NOORD
	BOB MCISSAC
	KELLY PETERSON
	MELVIN GEDDES
	GILBERT RUSSELL
	ROB ESHELBY
	JEANETTE JOUDREY
New York Fixer	JOHN LEONARD
New York Camera Assistant	JASON HARVEY
New York Production Assistant	MOIRA DEMOS

POST PRODUCTION

Assistant Editor	CHRISTINE CAMPBELL
Trainee Editor	T'AI ZIMMER
Dubbing Mixer	DAVE HUMPHRIES
Assistant Dubbing Mixer	ALAN SALLABANK
Sound Editor	KEVIN BRAZIER
	STEPHEN GRIFFITHS
Foley Artists	JOHN FEWELL
	JULIE ANKERSON
Video Effects	JASON FARROW at BLUE
Titles	MARTIN BUTTERWORTH
Music Mixer	STEVE PARR
Music Fixer	ISOBEL GRIFFITHS
Orchestration	DAVID LYON
Lyrics & Vocals	CARLTON
	JOHN HARRIS
Drums	CLIVE DEAMER
Piano	JOHN BAGGOT
String Arranger	SIMON HALE

Read the best of British screenwriting from ScreenPress Books:

THE FULL MONTY

Simon Beaufoy

The Full Monty opened in the summer of 1997 and by the spring of 1998 had become the most successful UK box-office release of all time.

This heart-warming and hilarious screenplay contains the complete shooting script to the film which includes a number of scenes that didn't make it to the finished movie.

Illustrated throughout with stills from the film.

ISBN 1 901680 02 9

Paperback, 162pp

£7.99

SLIDING DOORS

Peter Howitt

Sliding Doors begins with the dreadful day in the life of Helen, a successful PR executive fired from work, and develops into a fascinating exploration of the nature of destiny.

Intelligently weaving two stories simultaneously Peter Howitt's perceptive and engaging script explores the intriguing question we often ask ourselves – 'What if?'

Illustrated throughout with stills from the film

ISBN 1 901680 13 4

Paperback, 160pp

£7.99